JOHN GIELGUD

BACKWARD GLANCES

Part One TIMES FOR REFLECTION
Part Two DISTINGUISHED COMPANY

LIMELIGHT EDITIONS
NEW YORK

First Limelight Edition July 1990

Copyright © John Gielgud 1972, 1989

Published by arrangement with Hodder and Stoughton Limited, London.

Parts of this book were first published in the United States as *Distinguished Company* in 1972, by Doubleday & Co. First published in its present edition by Hodder and Stoughton Limited in 1989.

Library of Congress Cataloging-in-Publication Data

Gielgud, John, Sir, 1904–
    Backward glances / John Gielgud.
      p. cm.
    Includes index.
    ISBN 0-87910-140-7
    1. Gielgud, John, Sir, 1904– . 2. Gielgud, John, Sir,
1904– —Friends and associates. 3. Actors–Great
Britain–Biography.
    I. Title.
    PN2598.G45A3   1990
    792'.028'092–dc20
    [B]
                              90-36754
                                CIP

To Gwen and Peggy,
my two dear and lovely Juliets

CONTENTS

LIST OF ILLUSTRATIONS

ACKNOWLEDGMENTS

I would like to thank Messrs Mander and Mitchenson for their invaluable help in supplying the illustrations.

I would also like to acknowledge Sotheby's for permission to reproduce the photograph of Edith Sitwell by Cecil Beaton, and the Radio Times Hulton Picture Library for the photograph of Elizabeth Bergner.

FOREWORD

In 1971, when I was acting at Chichester, I celebrated my fiftieth year as a professional player. During my leisure hours that summer I amused myself by concocting a small book of reminiscences, recalling a number of actors and actresses whom I had known and admired in my earlier years, but all of whom are now sadly dead.

Since that time I have written various tributes and short pieces for various newspapers and magazines, and now these seem to have accumulated over the years into quite a considerable number. Hodder & Stoughton have thought fit to wish to re-publish these in the form of one book, as well as to reprint my first autobiography *Early Stages* (1939) and a further book, *Stage Directions*, which I wrote in 1963. Both are now in paperback. With the help of Edward Thompson, an old friend (and my editor at Heinemann Educational Books who first published the other books), I have chosen and rearranged these later writing efforts of mine into a collected shape.

The second part of this book is a direct reprint of my third book *Distinguished Company* (1972). The first part contains the various pieces, all connected with the theatre (but some only distantly so), and I am giving the whole book the title of *Backward Glances*, which I hope may convey an appropriate summary of its contents.

I have also to thank the original publishers who have allowed me to rescue many of the new excerpts from their archives.

JOHN GIELGUD, Wotton Underwood, August 1988

TIMES FOR REFLECTION

1

EDITH EVANS: A GREAT ACTRESS

How shall we best remember her? As heavenly Rosalind, or the lumbering peasant that was Juliet's Nurse? As one of her 'lovelies' as she used to call them: Millamant, Mrs Sullen, Daphne Laureola, Orinthia in *The Apple Cart*? Or as one of the working women she drew so well – the maid Gwenny in *The Late Christopher Bean*, and her two great performances on film, as the saviour of the village in *The Last Days of Dolwyn* and the crazy old lady in *The Whisperers*?

I first saw her act when I was a schoolboy towards the end of the 1914 war. Then she was playing supporting parts in various long-forgotten plays – spinsters, companions and even mothers in white wigs. The dragonfly had not yet emerged from the cocoon.

The eccentric William Poel had discovered her, and cast her as Cressida (after rehearsing her first in several male parts in the same production). It was he who encouraged her to leave the Belgravia hat shop in which she had been working and become a professional actress.

At that time she was considered plain, and leading ladies were expected to be beautiful, as they usually were. (Whether they could act as well was of course another matter.) Edith Evans was no beauty in the conventional sense. Her eyes, with their heavy lids, one set slightly lower than the other, gave her face an enigmatic originality. It was a fascinating canvas on which she soon learned to paint any character she chose.

In 1923 she was offered the showy part of a pork-packing Duchess with a gigolo in the original West End production of Somerset Maugham's *Our Betters*. But she turned it down, saying she refused to be typed in vapid society roles, and decided instead to go to Birmingham, where she triumphed as the Serpent (doubling with the She-Ancient) in Shaw's *Back to Methuselah* pentateuch. In her next big part, as Millamant in Congreve's *Way of the World* under Nigel Playfair at the Lyric, Hammersmith, she took the town by storm. It was a unique and exquisite performance. She purred and challenged, mocked and melted, showing her changing moods by the subtle shifting angles of her head, neck and shoulders. Poised and cool, she stood like a porcelain figure in a vitrine, as she handled her fan (though she never deigned to open it) in the great love scene, using it for attack or defence, now coquettishly pointing it upwards beneath her chin, now resting it languidly against her cheek, while the words flowed on, phrasing and diction balanced in perfect cadences, as she smiled and pouted to deliver her delicious sallies.

She showed her superb taste by brilliant timing and control, never stooping to indulge an over-enthusiastic audience, and disdaining any temptation to overstress an emotional moment or allow too many laughs to interrupt the pace of a comic scene.

Only tragedy eluded her, and this was perhaps because her nature was essentially sunny and resilient, besides which her voice, however athletic and articulate, lacked deep notes that she could sustain in her lower register. She always refused to attempt Lady Macbeth, whose explicit admission of evil she could not bring herself to accept. She grew to hate her success as Lady Bracknell, though it was perhaps the most popular and famous of all her great impersonations. She was staying at my cottage in Essex one weekend just before the war when I suggested a possible revival of the Wilde play. I took a copy from the bookshelf and we read the bag scene together to the guests. After the hysterical laughter had died down, Edith handed me back the book and remarked gravely, 'I know those women. They ring the bell and tell you to put a lump of coal on.' But in the end she had to play the part too often – in a film, for the gramophone and on radio, as well as for several long runs in the theatre, and she firmly refused my entreaties to repeat it in New York. She disliked the imitations of her trumpet tone in the famous 'A HANDBAG?' which many people seemed to think was the alpha and omega of her performance as Lady Bracknell. For me there was so much else to admire, exquisite details of observation and execution. The sly look of suspicion, for instance, as she glanced at the armchair she had chosen for the first interview with Worthing in the first act. In those few seconds she managed to convey both appraisal and approval, to reassure herself of the suitability of that particular piece of furniture before it should enthrone her corseted dignity as she lowerered herself into the seat.

She disliked the trappings of a great star, the gossip, the private anecdotes made public, the intrigue, scandal and petty-mindedness. One always felt one must approach her with respect and restraint. She hated gush, was wary of strangers and conventional compliments, striving to create her performances from an inner conviction, trying to find the 'bridges', as she called them, to achieve progression and climax in the characters she was determined to bring to life. 'I never make effects,' she used to say. Of course she did, but with what subtlety, skill and artistry she set about it.

In 1929 I first acted with her, for only a few weeks, in a play about Florence Nightingale called *The Lady with the Lamp*, and she advised me then to go to the Old Vic, a decision which was to further my career to unexpected advantage.

Three years later I was asked to direct (for the first time) by the young undergraduates of the OUDS, a production of *Romeo and Juliet* at Oxford, a play I already knew and loved, and found myself enriched by the privilege of working with Peggy Ashcroft as Juliet and Edith Evans as the Nurse. Of course I was greatly in awe of her at first. I timidly suggested that she might perhaps be doing needlework in her opening scene with Juliet and Lady Capulet. I pictured her, I suppose, with a tapestry in a frame and a large needle threading in and out, typical romantic costume play 'business'. I was quite wrong. She kept a tiny piece of material between her hands which she handled very sparingly (almost hiding it in her long sleeves), using a gentle rhythmic movement to give a slight counterpoint to her first long speech without in the least detracting from it. It was my first glimpse of her remarkable instinct for selectivity.

She seemed to prefer to move very little. I do not remember any swift entrances or exits in her performances, but she taught me to give up my own impatient inclination to drive actors about the stage in order to give a scene excitement long before the dialogue demanded it. You could not hurry her or muddle her with too many suggestions before she was ready for them. The character and its truth, the pattern of the syllables, the give and take of the vocal exchanges – these were slowly taking shape during the early rehearsals, and from these basic foundations she began to develop her performance. She governed her audiences and refused to woo them, though her wooing scenes as Millamant, Rosalind, Orinthia, were miracles of coquetry and provocation. She was baleful in *The Old Ladies* and *The Witch of Edmonton*, overwhelmingly touching in simple characters – as the Welsh housemaid in *The Late Christopher Bean* for instance. She could be aristocratic (and absurdly autocratic) as Lady Bracknell, and equally well bred (and even sometimes ridiculous) in *The Chalk Garden* when her brilliant technical skill never failed to fascinate me. As she heard of her butler's death in the last act, I never tired of watching her as she switched from comedy to pathos and back again in the course of a scene of only a few lines.

She had real humility. I could feel this even in the honest reluctance with which she took her curtain calls – a polite but restrained acknowledgment of the applause, with none of the affectation or smugness which sometimes mar the behaviour of lesser artists on these occasions. She had enormous authority but also intrinsic shyness. Not until the part she was rehearsing really possessed her would she completely sweep in to her performance. She could not, as actors sometimes do, patch together material tried out successfully in other plays, in order to achieve a superficial shortcut to a new creation.

I think she found it difficult to expose her feelings in private life, and she was reluctant to give opinions unless she felt them with great certainty. She had no wish to be misquoted by making unconsidered or hasty remarks. About the acting of her colleagues she was always extremely reticent, though praise from her was as precious as it was rare. I was never sure just how much she was aware of what was going on around her on the stage. Admittedly she was supremely self-centred, but she was neither selfish nor jealous, though occasionally prim and narrow. Strong but uncertain of herself, formidable yet easily melting, proud yet meek, she was an extraordinary mixture. She sometimes longed to lead an ordinary life, to dance and skate and lark, to be a housewife, to look after a husband, to cook and farm and live in the country, but her talent for acting was too strong to enable her to succeed anywhere but in the theatre. She was inclined to defy tradition (though of course she created it herself). No chestnuts for her about Mrs Siddons and Mrs Bracegirdle, no reading up of old stage 'business'. I remember her being quite sarcastic at the grandeur of Bernhardt's dressing-room and large bathroom when she occupied it in Paris where we once played together. She always liked to boast of her early apprenticeship in the West End ('I never had to tour and get into all those bad habits!') with Dennis Eadie, Charles Hawtrey and Gerald du Maurier, whose fine manners and professional courtesy she always quoted with admiration.

She hated slovenliness, unpunctuality, rudeness and careless talk. She disliked extravagance, had a reputation for stinginess, but did many generous actions in strictest secrecy. She tried as far as possible to divide her own life and her life in the theatre into completely separate compartments. I do not think she had more than a dozen intimate friends. Her letters were few, but one felt proud to receive one, knowing that it cost her an effort to put pen to paper. She was often witty and pungent, and could be great fun if she was in the mood. But she was intensely fastidious and abhorred cheapness either in talk or action.

She once paid me a sublime compliment which I shall always cherish. 'Your Benedick, Johnnie,' she said once, after a rather stormy argument we had had about the playing of comedy, 'that performance you know, was seven-eighths perfection!'

The *Observer*, 17th October 1976

2

SYBIL THORNDIKE: A GREAT WOMAN

In 1922 she came to the RADA and rehearsed our class in scenes from the *Medea*. She had sandy hair in those days, arranged in coils round her ears, like radio receivers, and wore long straight dresses in bright colours with strings of beads round her neck. She told me that Jason was a self-righteous prig and I must play him so. She exuded vitality, enthusiasm, generosity, and we were all spell-bound as we listened to her.

I do not remember seeing her on the stage until *Saint Joan* in 1924, when I was lucky enough to be at the opening night, sitting with my parents in the dress circle of the New Theatre. It was an inspiring occasion – play, production, décor, acting, it all seemed perfect to me – and, at the end of the evening, when Sybil Thorndike led on the weary actors to take a dozen calls, all of them suddenly looking utterly exhausted by the strain of the long performance, I realised, perhaps for the first time, something of the agonies and triumphs of theatrical achievement.

She was surely the best-loved English actress since Ellen Terry, and these two great players shared many of the same fine qualities – generosity, diligence, modesty, simplicity. Both were demons for hard work – Ellen Terry called it her blessèd work, but that could be taken with two different meanings, for like Edith she often longed (or said she longed) to live in the country and forget the theatre. But her own private life was not destined to bring her great happiness, and she was to become, alas, a somewhat tragic figure in her old age.

It was quite otherwise with Sybil Thorndike. The theatre was the breath of life to her – the theatre, music, and her deep religious faith. Blessed with immense talent, boundless energy, unremitting application and splendid health – until the last few years when she learned to triumph over continual pain and increasing disabilities – she fought her way, helped by the devotion of a brilliant husband and loving family, to worldwide recognition. Her good works were manifold, her influence for good shone from her like a beacon, but she hated to be praised and to be thought sweet and saintly. 'I hate pathos,' she said once. 'It's soft and weak. But tragedy has fight.' And in Lewis Casson she had a superb partner and a tremendous fighter, though his temperament was often inclined to be moody and pessimistic in contrast to Sybil's radiant determination to see the best in everyone and everything around her. He argued with her endlessly, criticised her ruthlessly, and tried to control some of the more eccentric enthusiasms and outbursts of exaggeration which sometimes tended to mar her acting. Outrageous she could certainly be at times, playing to the hilt some second-rate vehicle which gave her an opportunity to let off steam in some particularly repulsive or wildly melodramatic character. But Sybil would be the first to admit, with a hoot of laughter, that it was all such fun, and apologise ruefully for overacting at a matinée with the excuse that a cherished grandchild had been in front.

In her long life there was no moment wasted, never a thought of boredom, laziness or surfeit. She and Lewis cared little for money, clothes, rich food or social grandeur, though they were perfectly willing to enjoy such things occasionally when they came their way. Sybil, someone said once, had no airs, only graces. She could be perfectly at ease with Royalty, poets, politicians or men of letters, and equally natural sitting on the doorstep of a miner's cottage in Wales, chatting to the wives and telling them the story of Medea. But you would hardly expect to find her at Wimbledon or Ascot – more probably at home, doing piano scales and voice exercises, learning a new part, studying a new language, reading aloud to her grandchildren, or arguing furiously with Lewis.

Intensely feminine in her maternal and womanly qualities, she could not on the stage be coquettish or swooningly romantic. During the Great War she played several male parts in Shakespeare at the Old Vic and found the experience a thrilling one, but she never attempted Juliet or Cleopatra. 'I can't be sheer femininity,' she said. 'Feminine wiles I can't manage and I don't want to!'

Both she and Lewis had a passion for words. Fanatical about speech, rhythms, phrasing, diction and modulation, they were inspired disciples of Poel, Granville–Barker, Shaw, Gilbert Murray and their voice-coach, Elsie Fogerty.

She was very fine, though to my mind unequal, in her playing of tragedy, but she was one of the few actresses of her generation who dared even to attempt it. She took the stage, whether in Lady Macbeth, Queen Katharine or Hecuba, with a splendid stride, faultless phrasing and diction, and riveted her audiences with superb authority and vocal power. In comedy she was sometimes tempted to hit too hard, but, as the years passed her skill and control, under Lewis' iron hand, restrained and refined the execution of her art to a marked degree.

Saint Joan of course was written for her, and it was her acting masterpiece, though she must have got sick and tired of hearing people say so. Her performance was unrivalled. Here she did not need to play for sheer femininity, nor for masculinity either. Her tearing up of the recantation in the trial scene was a moment of really great acting that I shall never forget, but she was equally convincing in the slangy colloquial passages as in the great poetic speeches, blending the different sides of the character with unerring judgement, and never for a moment allowing sentimentality or sanctimoniousness to intrude on the simple directness of her attitude.

In her private life she managed somehow to retain a certain reserve and dignity, despite an ebullient façade. She had beautiful manners. Genuinely interested in everyone she met, strangers as well as friends, she could bounce and flounce without ever losing her modesty and basic humility. And the moment you were lucky enough to work with her in the theatre, you knew she was a leader, a giver, not self-centred – professional to her fingertips, disciplined, punctual, kind. She confessed to having a terrible temper but I never saw a sign of it myself.

To me the most perfect examples of her acting were in some of the comparatively restrained characters in which she displayed her essential womanliness. Jane Clegg, Miss Moffat in *The Corn is Green*, Mother parts in *The Distaff Side* and *The Linden Tree*, and her lovely performances in the two Hunter plays, *Waters of the Moon* and *A Day by the Sea*. 'When Lewis died,' she said, 'I became a bit tired of myself.' But we could never tire of her as we watched her rallying her forces in those last splendid years, still eager to understand new styles, appreciate new talents, to lend shrewd advice and criticism, fearlessly honest about everything she saw and read.

Her beauty grew, as it had every right to do, in her old age, and her noble head, veiled in the white silk scarf she came to wear always, picked her out in any gathering, whether at theatres or parties or in church, as she listened and watched and walked, more slowly now, with an unerring sense of any occasion she was honouring with her presence. During these last years, it was sad to see her the victim of continual pain. But how magnificently she rose above it. 'My piffling arthritis,' she would say. With what unforgettable dignity she led her family up the long nave of the Abbey at the memorial service for her husband. How eagerly she followed every moment of the service, and how like her to wait afterwards to greet a great crowd of friends. One day not long afterwards I called on her at her flat in Chelsea to find her sitting in an armchair, reading Sir Thomas More. On another I found her lying on her bed, evidently in great pain. 'A bit tired today,' she said, 'for it was Lewis' anniversary yesterday, so I got them to drive me up to Golders Green and sat there for half an hour.' But she announced defiantly that she intended to come to see me in Pinter's *No Man's Land* the following week. I begged her not to make the effort and thought no more about it, but when the evening came, sure enough, during the interval, I heard over the loud-speaker, above the chatter of the audience, her voice, unmistakably clear: 'Do you know my daughter-in-law Patricia?' Ralph Richardson bounded into my dressing-room. 'She's here after all', and of course we both had letters afterwards. George Devine told me that she came to see every one of the new plays he was then presenting at the Court, and would always write him vivid and constructive criticism as soon as she got home.

How fitting that her very last public appearance should have been at the Old Vic on its farewell night when, at the end of the performance, she was wheeled down the aisle in her chair to smile and wave for the last time to the people sitting in the theatre she had always loved so well.

Lively and personal, passionate and argumentative, always practising her piano, cooking her dinner, making her bed, travelling, acting, learning a new language or a new poem, simple clothes, simple tastes, a magnificent wife and mother – surely one of the rarest women of our time.

'O Lewis,' she cried once, 'if only we could be the first actors to play on the moon.'

The *Sunday Times*, 13th June 1976

3

RALPH RICHARDSON: A GREAT GENTLEMAN, A RARE SPIRIT

He was my friend, faithful and just to me,
But Brutus says he was ambitious . . .

But Ralph was not, I think, a predominantly ambitious man, except in his lifelong determination to perfect his art. He was never satisfied with a single one of his performances, but would go on working to improve what would seem to me a perfect interpretation, however often repeated, until the very last time he came to play it.

Besides cherishing our long years of work together in the theatre, where he was such an inspiring and generous partner, I grew to love him in private life as a great gentleman, a rare spirit, fair and balanced, devotedly loyal and tolerant and, as a companion, bursting with vitality, curiosity and humour.

A consummate craftsman, endlessly painstaking in every detail where his work was concerned, he was something of a perfectionist in many fields outside the theatre. He read voraciously. Two or three different books – a novel, a classic, a biography, a thriller – these would, during a long run, be propped up on shelves and tables for him to peruse during his waits in the dressing-room. His beautiful houses were filled with furniture, ornaments and pictures which reflected his unerring individual taste.

He loved to discuss his motorbikes and cars, his clocks and

pets, to argue about films and plays he had been to see. He never cared for gossip, and would avoid, if possible, giving adverse criticism of other players, though he could tell a good actor at a glance and shrewdly sum up an indifferent one equally quickly. He was a wonderful influence in a company, punctual, concentrated and completely professional, patient and courteous in delays and crises, critical (and intensely self-critical) and never malicious, taking his own time to consider questions and answering them patiently with grace and wisdom.

On the very few occasions when I saw him in a rage, he suddenly showed a formidable strength, but the mood would quickly pass, and he never harboured grudges.

When we first acted together at the Old Vic in 1930, I little thought that we might be friends. At first we were inclined to circle round each other like suspicious dogs. In our opening production I played Hotspur to his Prince Hal, and was relieved, though somewhat surprised, to discover that he was as reluctant as I to engage in the swordplay demanded in the later under-rehearsed scenes at Shrewsbury. On the first night I was amazed at his whispered instructions – surely, I thought, the audience must hear them too – 'Now you hit me, cocky. Now I hit you.'

A few weeks later, as we moved into rehearsals for *The Tempest*, I rather hesitatingly ventured to suggest to him a private session for examining one of our scenes together, and he immediately agreed with the greatest modesty and good humour. This was, as he has often said himself, the beginning of a friendship that was to last for fifty years.

There are many things about me that he must have found deeply unsympathetic, but his sensitive generosity has never faltered. When we ventured into the avant-garde together in *Home* and *No Man's Land* we both felt we were paddling dangerously in uncharted seas, but our shared success in both plays was a lively encouragement as well as a refreshing challenge after the more conventional ups and downs of our past careers.

I think he was fundamentally a shy man, and in his later years he cultivated a certain delightfully eccentric vagueness, especially when he was cornered by strangers or failed to greet someone he had not noticed. Once, when an understudy, whom he had never seen before, went on for one of the two supporting parts in *No Man's Land*, Ralph absentmindedly congratulated a stagehand who happened to be standing near him after the curtain fell.

But actually he was intensely observant and extremely farseeing. He warmed immediately to a sympathetic author, or to a new director whom he decided to trust – Lindsay Anderson, for instance, Peter Hall and, I am proud to say, myself. He was never jealous or spiteful, never bitter or attempting to blame anyone but himself after his occasional failures, always eager to set to work on the next venture, fighting his gradual difficulties in learning a complicated new text by writing it out in huge letters with coloured chalks and pinning it on boards all round his study walls.

He could give delightfully comical advice. 'How many clubs do you belong to, Ralph?' I once asked him. 'Three,' he replied. 'But, you know, you should never go to the same club more than once a week.' 'Aren't your subscription bills rather heavy?' 'Oh, I just write out a banker's order.'

How sadly I shall miss his cheerful voice on the telephone, telling me of a new book he had just finished reading (a copy would arrive by the next post) and his patience with my chattering tongue. When we appeared together on talk shows in America, his pauses and slowness would make me nervous and, fearing to bore the listeners, I would break into a torrent of anecdote which I kept trying to control lest he should think I was trying to steal the show. But he would cap my gabble brilliantly with a look and a short comment, well-considered, which threw the ball back into his own court with unerring skill and deftness. When I was directing him in a play he learnt most cleverly how to make use of the few good suggestions I made at a rehearsal and discard the many bad ones.

One of the few arguments I ever had with him was over his first entrance in *The School for Scandal*, as Sir Peter Teazle. Ralph argued every day, and we could not begin to rehearse the scene. 'Should I have a newspaper in my hand? A walking-stick? Or be taking snuff perhaps?' At last one morning he leaned across the footlights and said, 'You know, Johnnie, I prayed to God last night to tell me how to come on in this opening scene. And this morning God answered, "Do what it says in the text, just come on."'

The loss of a most dear friend is only equalled by the loss of him as a great man of the English theatre. His Falstaff, Peer Gynt, the drunken actor in *Eden End*, Borkman, *Early Days*, all these superb performances, as well as those in plays and films when we have appeared together, are unforgettable memories for me and will always remain so. I hope the happiness of his married life and the great successes and popularity which he achieved, especially in his later years, consoled and gratified him after the long struggle he won so patiently in the early days of his career.

The *Observer*, 16th October 1983

4

ELIZABETH BERGNER

Elfin-like, volatile, mischievous, fascinating. Elizabeth Bergner had all these qualities. But the huge public that had raved over her performance in Margaret Kennedy's *Escape Me Never* in 1934, both in London and New York, took little notice of her death in 1987. Only one or two actors besides myself were present at her funeral, though the German Government had sent a huge wreath, as well as rewarding her with the Duse Memorial shield, during her last years, evidence that she was still gratefully remembered in the country which she had been one of the first actresses to leave when Hitler came to power. But though she often talked in her last days of going back to live in Berlin or Vienna, she remained and died in London.

I had a long and unforgettable friendship with her, though I could never be certain of her moods. She had been a great star, with all the spoilt trappings of a gifted celebrity, from the time of her earliest successes on the continent – some under Max Rheinhardt – and I was not altogether surprised to read, in Count Kessler's memoirs, that during a performance of *Romeo and Juliet* (with Franz Lederer and Elizabeth) the manager had come before the curtain to announce that Miss Bergner was so exhausted by the big scene she had just played that there would have to be a short interval to enable her to recover her energies – a somewhat unusual emergency it seemed to me.

In 1934 I met her, just before she first appeared in London, at Boulestin's Restaurant, when Emlyn Williams and I had asked her to lunch with us to suggest she might star in *Spring*

1600, a play of Emlyn's which I was about to direct. It was, of course, an idiotic idea, as the leading character was an English country girl, and her accent would have been an impossible barrier, but we were fascinated by her all the same.

She cleverly chose C. B. Cochran to sponsor her début in England, as he was to do years later in *The Boy David*. Komisarjevsky, who directed her in both plays, told me that on the first night in Manchester (of *Escape Me Never*) he had to push her on to the stage from the wings, since she was paralysed with nervousness. But when I saw the play one afternoon in London, she acted enchantingly, but spoilt her most dramatic scene in the last act by giggling, though this did not seem to deter the audience from wild applause and endless curtain calls at the end of the performance. As I walked down Shaftesbury Avenue afterwards, I heard a tremendous roar behind me, and, looking round, I saw an open taxi slowly driving along, and Elizabeth sitting on the hood with flowers in her lap, waving to a mass of shouting fans who were following her, crowding the pavements on both sides of the street.

Her husband, Paul Czinner, directed all the films in which she starred with great réclame: *Escape Me Never, Catherine the Great*, and a better forgotten *As You Like It*. Her German-speaking film *Der Träumende Mund*, had already been seen by cinema buffs in London, who praised it greatly and all the English film and stage critics (except James Agate, who always pugnaciously refused her his approval and dismissed her as being 'mousey-pousey') were unanimous in extolling her talents to the skies.

She forfeited her popularity, however, when, at the outbreak of the war, she was to be one of the stars in a film of Michael Powell's, *49th Parallel*. The scenes she was in demanded some days on location in Canada, but after a few days she suddenly threw up her part and fled to Hollywood, with the result that the whole sequence had to be scrapped and reshot with Glynis Johns. (Gracie Fields, who left for the States at about the same time with her new husband, Monty Banks, became equally unpopular in consequence – the mill girls in Lancashire were even said to have broken all her gramophone records – but she reinstated herself a few years later at a huge concert at the Albert Hall – in which I made a short appearance – under the auspices of Basil Dean, who was then to direct her in several successful films.)

Meanwhile, in California, Elizabeth made an English film version of *Der Träumende Mund* (Dreaming Lips), and *A Stolen Life* with Michael Redgrave, and remained in America for several years. She acted in a sex melodrama *The Two Mrs Carrolls* on the Subway Circuit, and appeared in New York, for a short run, in an ill-conceived version of *The Duchess of Malfi*, adapted by W. H. Auden, and directed by George Rylands of Cambridge, who came over (with Arthur Marshall as assistant). The cast included a black actor, Canada Lee, as Bosola, playing in white face!

Czinner had bought the scenery and costumes we had used in our production of the play in London the year before, but Elizabeth commissioned new costumes for herself and gave Peggy Ashcroft's dresses to the ladies-in-waiting.

She lived for some time in Princeton, renewing friendships with Brecht, Einstein, Mann and other distinguished European refugees, but I could never persuade her to talk about them, or even to tell me stories of her early triumphs before she came to England.

She flattered me greatly when, in 1937, she asked me to direct *The Boy David*, which Barrie, who had fallen in love with her, had written especially for her, but I could not care for the play when I was sent it to read. When Elizabeth came to my flat to dine with me and discuss the matter, I hedged at criticising the text of the great man, but said I would only consider the task she offered me if I could count on her support in suggesting changes. But at this point, Elizabeth broke a string of beads which she was wearing round her neck and dived under the sofa to retrieve them, and I at once made up my mind to doubt the likelihood of her using any influence on my behalf, and demurred at the responsibility of working with such eminent seniors as Cochran, Barrie, and Augustus John, who was to design the décor. Barrie died just before the London opening and the production was postponed, after a try-out in Edinburgh, when Elizabeth fired the director, H. K. Ayliff, and temporarily retired into a nursing home. When she emerged, Komisarjevsky was engaged to re-direct, and Ernest Stern and the Motleys were brought in for the scenery and costumes. But the play was damned by the London critics and lasted at His Majesty's for only a few weeks, despite a fine cast, including Godfrey Tearle, Ion Swinley, Sir John Martin-Harvey and Jean Cadell. Elizabeth made her entrance on a donkey and was said to have amused herself by crouching at Tearle's feet and pulling hairs out of his leg to make him laugh.

Barrie had left a legacy to Elizabeth in his will, and there was some rather spiteful speculation in the press at his neglect of the leading ladies who had played Peter Pan in so many years of successful revivals. Elizabeth told me this episode had upset and embarrassed her very much. But she would also boast of her behaviour at a matinée of *Saint Joan* at Malvern when she got bored and proceeded to cut the famous Bells speech, unaware that Shaw was in the audience. 'He came round,' she said, 'and threw the book at me.' 'What on earth did you do, Elizabeth?' I enquired. 'I threw it back,' she replied with her inimitable giggle.

When she finally reappeared in London after many years, she rashly chose for her vehicle a translation of Molière's *Malade Imaginaire*, which failed completely, though she had some fun in trying to upstage the redoubtable old warhorse A. E. Matthews, who was far too experienced a performer to let her get away with it. She could be very unpredictable as a colleague, though enchantingly courteous towards players she admired. Irene Vanbrugh and Leon Quartermaine were both devoted to her, and the young Irene Worth, who acted with her when she was quite a beginner, and was later to become an intimate friend, told me how much she had learned from working with her.

After Paul Czinner's death she continued to live in her elegant flat in Eaton Square, where she had nursed him devotedly through a long illness. She had recently become a Christian Scientist, and at her cremation service the ceremony was half Scientist and half Jewish.

I only acted with her once myself in a television version of Shaw's *In Good King Charles's Golden Days* when I had suggested her for the part of Catherine of Braganza, who has a charming scene with the King in the epilogue (the part had been created in the theatre by Irene Vanbrugh, who must have been almost as unsuitably cast as Ernest Thesiger, who played the King). Elizabeth gave an exquisite performance, though she was difficult and evasive during the rehearsals, begging me to rehearse alone with her without the director, suggesting cuts and transpositions, and avoiding meeting the other members of the cast, and she never referred to the episode again. But she was an intensely generous friend, always giving me valuable presents, but very difficult to please when I tried to think of suitable tokens in return – flowers seemed to annoy her, though her drawing-room always seemed packed with flowers, books, and cards, though she did seem to like a present of chocolates. But she was apt to keep her friends in separate boxes – Irene Worth, Michael Redgrave, and myself, for instance, whom she would never invite together. Increasing deafness, I think, made her reluctant to entertain more than one person at a time. Usually wearing horn-rimmed spectacles, with grey hair not touched up, and dressed in exceedingly becoming trouser-suits, beautifully simple and well cut, she was still the most delightful and attractive hostess.

Quite often she would go back to Germany, to act there in *The Deep Blue Sea* by Terence Rattigan, and the Shaw-Campbell duologue *Dear Liar*, as well as a number of films, few of which were shown in this country. But she seemed to find little pleasure in these visits, and seemed to long to appear again on the London stage, though I tried in vain to interest her in plays that I thought might suit her (one especially: *La Monstre Sacrée* of Cocteau). But she had no use for any of them.

Meanwhile she booked seats – always in the front row so that she could hear better – for concerts and plays of all kinds, and she read voraciously and took enormous interest in the experimental theatre, as well as in films, museums and picture exhibitions. She talked of playing in a new piece at the Royal Court but turned it down in the end. Then she appeared in a translation of a Hungarian play called *Cat's Play* at the Greenwich Theatre, in which she was helped through by the director, Robin Phillips, and in which she was brilliant as ever, but very unpleasant to the distinguished actress with whom she had important scenes to play. This last appearance in London made very little stir. Finally, she decided – also at Greenwich (where evidently her remarkable gifts had not gone unappreciated), to play the drug-taking wife in Eugine O'Neill's sequel to *Long Day's Journey Into Night*, called *Fading Mansions*. But in the rehearsals of this play she proved so undisciplined that it was decided to drop her from the cast, and another actress was secretly engaged. I was dismayed to be the person to break this news to her, but to my amazement she shrugged the insult off, and went into roars of laughter at the news. I could not help admiring her remarkable courage in facing old age and losing her great reputation, and I continued to visit her quite often and sometimes I took her to the theatre. Then I was told, when I telephoned, that she had become very ill, and I never saw her again.

5

VIVIEN LEIGH

What seems to me most remarkable, as far as her career was concerned, was her steady determination to be a fine stage actress, to make her career in the living theatre, when, with her natural beauty, skill, and grace of movement, gifts which were of course invaluable in helping to create the magic of her personality, she could so easily have stayed aloof and supreme in her unique position as a screen actress. Of course she will always be remembered as Scarlett O'Hara, as Lady Hamilton, and later for her wonderful acting in the *Streetcar* film. But these screen successes by no means satisfied her ambitions, and she had a lifelong devotion to the theatre, and determined to work there diligently through the years in order to reach the heights which she afterwards achieved. Though in her first big success, *The Mask of Virtue*, she had taken the critics and public by storm, she knew that her youth and beauty were the chief factors of her immediate success, and she was modest and shrewd enough to face the challenge of developing herself so as to find the widest possible range of which she was capable.

Her marriage to Laurence Olivier was an inspiration to her qualities – not only as a devoted pupil but also as a brilliant partner. Her performance in their seasons together, not only at the St James's Theatre (whose untimely destruction she tried so gallantly to prevent), but also at the Old Vic and Stratford, and in tours all over the world – in Russia, Australia, Europe and America – added fresh laurels to her crown. Besides the classic parts, she delighted everyone too in the modern plays she chose, each of which made different demands upon her versatility – *The Skin of Our Teeth, The Sleeping Prince, Antigone*, and later *Duel of Angels*.

She had a charmingly distinctive voice. On the telephone one recognised it immediately – that touch of imperiousness, combined with a childlike eager warmth full of friendliness and gaiety. But she was determined to increase the range of it for the theatre, and in Shakespeare's Cleopatra, in which I thought she gave her finest classical performance, she succeeded in lowering her whole register from the natural pitch she was using as the little girl Cleopatra in Shaw's play – a remarkable feat which few actresses could have sustained as successfully as she did. Her Lady Macbeth, too, showed an astonishing vocal power and poignancy of feeling – and it is a thousand pities that the project of filming her performance of this was abandoned, for I believe it would have created worldwide admiration.

Her manners both in the theatre and in private life were always impeccable. She was punctual, modest, and endlessly thoughtful and considerate. She was frank without being unkind, elegant but never ostentatious. Her houses were as lovely as her beautiful and simple clothes. Whenever she was not entirely absorbed in the theatre she was endlessly busy, decorating her rooms, planning surprises for her friends, giving advice on her garden, entertaining lavishly but always with the utmost grace and selectivity.

I had never thought to become an intimate friend of hers. My first meeting with her was at Oxford in 1937, when she played the little queen in *Richard the Second* with the students. I was acting in London at the time, and so only met her when I was directing the rehearsals. The part is not a very interesting one, though she managed to endow it with every possible grace of speech and movement, and wore her medieval costumes with consummate charm – but I never got to know her in these days.

A few years later, during the war, I acted with her in *The Doctor's Dilemma*, when another actor was taken ill, and from that time we began an acquaintanceship which slowly ripened into a deep friendship and affection, and it is a wonderful happiness to me that during her last years I had the joy of seeing her so often and came to love her so well.

Of course she was restless and drove herself too hard. Although she seemed so astonishingly resilient, she often suffered ill health and fits of great depression, but she made light of the fact and rarely admitted to it or talked about it to other people. Her courage in the face of personal unhappiness was touching and remarkable. She always spoke affectionately of those who had first recognised her talents and helped her to develop her natural gifts. She studied and experimented continually, and always brought to rehearsal a willingness and technical flexibility which was the result of unceasing self-criticism and devotion to her work.

As she grew older she acquired a new kind of beauty, without any need of artifice, and she seemed to harbour no resentment against the competition of younger beautiful women. She was always enormously interested in everything, people, places, changes of fashion – and she had friends of every different sort and kind in London, in her country homes and in America and Australia. How delightfully she would talk of her Japanese admirers, who wrote her such charmingly phrased letters, and of those in Russia, where her film *Waterloo Bridge* is still considered a classic. She had the most punctilious and gracious way of answering letters and of dealing with strangers, admirers, newspaper men and women, and she was loved in the theatres she worked in for her sweetness to staff and company alike.

Her magic quality was unique. A great beauty, a natural star, a consummate screen actress and a versatile and powerful personality in the theatre – she had a range that could stretch from the comedy Sabina in *Skin of Our Teeth* to the naturalistic agonies of Blanche DuBois in *Streetcar*, and the major demands of Lady Macbeth and Cleopatra. Even in *Titus Andronicus*, when she had only a few short scenes, she contrived the most beautiful pictorial effects. Who can forget the macabre grace with which she guided the staff with her elbows to write in the sand with it, a ravished victim gliding across the stage in her long grey robe.

We who loved her must be always thankful for knowing

her and working with her, and salute her for all she gave the world, so generously and so gaily.

Now boast thee, Death, in thy possession lies
A lass unparallel'd.

6

GWEN FFRANGCON-DAVIES

In the early Nineteen Twenties, when I first came to know her, she was already something of a cult personality in the London theatre, to which she had graduated, after an improbable apprenticeship touring in musical comedy successes, to establish herself as leading lady of Sir Barry Jackson's repertory company at Birmingham. Daughter of a fine and well-known singer father, her success at the Glastonbury Festival in Rutland Boughton's opera, *The Immortal Hour*, led Sir Barry to present her in London in the same part – the fairy princess Etain – at the Regent Theatre, opposite King's Cross Station (long pulled down) for a short season, to be followed by a production of *Romeo and Juliet*, in which, after several nerve-wracking auditions, I was finally engaged, as a nineteen year old novice, to play Romeo – Gwen had already played the part with success in Birmingham.

I do not believe Gwen herself was present at my auditions, and I had to deliver my speeches, in a large empty auditorium, to Sir Barry and his director, H. K. Ayliff (a tall, grim figure with a toupée, dressed in green tweeds and brown boots) while a stage-manager fed me from the wings with Juliet's lines. Gwen afterwards told me that she had seen me as the Poet Butterfly in Capek's *The Insect Play* – my first professional engagement in London two years before – and thought me disastrously bad. Consequently she was dismayed to hear I was to partner her. (She evidently had not been consulted in the matter herself.)

However, after a few days' rehearsal she decided to put up with me, and helped and encouraged me in every possible

way, though my performance was very inadequate, and the
production, a rather chilly affair except for Gwen's enchanting
Botticelli Juliet, greatly praised by a few discerning critics
and her growing band of devoted admirers, only lasted for a
few weeks, two of which I was to miss owing to illness. I
fainted one day during the balcony scene but managed to
finish the performance (and hoped that the audience might
have thought me to have swooned with lyrical ecstasy). My
understudy was incompetent, and Ion Swinley and Ernest
Milton were hastily summoned to replace me, for a week
each, which must have created a series of emergencies for all
concerned.

Throughout her long career, Gwen's skilful voice–control and
graceful movements, as well as her unusually talented gift
for wearing period costume, made her greatly in demand,
especially for Shakespeare. She appeared as Titania, Cordelia
and some years later as Ophelia, and the beautiful photographs
of her in those busy days show how great was her appealing
personality, though she never made claim to being a raving
beauty. Laura Knight painted her as Juliet as she stood in her
petticoat in the dressing-room, and when she played Isabella
the She-Wolf for the Phoenix Society's special performances
of Marlowe's *Edward the Second*, she was immortalised by
Walter Sickert in a magnificent portrait which now hangs
nobly in the Tate Gallery.

But she was equally successful in many contemporary
plays, including some of Shaw's best women's parts – Mrs
Dubedat, Eliza Doolittle, and the young Cleopatra when her
Caesar was Cedric Hardwicke, a partnership that was to
continue some years later, with great advantage to them both,
in *The Barretts of Wimpole Street*.

But one of my favourite memories of her is also in a Shaw
play, when she was Eve in the Garden of Eden scene in his
pentateuch *Back to Methuselah*, with Edith Evans as the hissing
Serpent. In the second part of this play she was the old Eve,
trying to cope with a rebellious Cain, and in this scene she
was movingly effective. Then, in the last Methuselah play,
she acted the Newly-Born, emerging from a huge property
egg and tottering about with bare feet in a long white nightie,
while Edith Evans appeared as the She-Ancient wearing a
bald wig and hideous rags. She and Gwen were to be cast in

plays together many times, and were devoted friends in private life, though I always felt that, in the theatre, Edith was inclined to under-rate Gwen's brilliant talents and was sometimes inclined to patronise her.

In 1928, Gwen and I acted together in a modern piece called *Prejudice* of which I remember little, save that I had to be Jewish, and Gwen a New England country girl, for which she assumed a most authentic-sounding accent. I had thought I was going to be very good, and was duly brought down from my high horse when, lying in bed after the first performance and eagerly sitting up to open the newspapers, I sank back on my pillow murmuring, 'Christ! Gwen's got the notices!'

But we remained as good friends as ever, and when, in 1932, after her triumph in *The Barretts*, I offered her the comparatively small part of the Queen, Anne of Bohemia, in *Richard of Bordeaux*, she accepted it eagerly, and her enchanting performance proved to be an invaluable contribution to the success of the play.

Her vivacity and enterprise led her to undertake a remarkable range of entirely different plays and characters. She played Tess in an adaptation of the Hardy novel, and she and Ion Swinley went down to the country and acted a scene from the play on the hearth rug in the great man's drawing-room. She was a Marseilles prostitute in *Maya* at the Gate Theatre Club (public performance banned by the Lord Chamberlain), a servant drudge, Elsie, in an adaptation of Arnold Bennett's *Riceyman Steps*, and Magda in a play by Sudermann which had been famous in the repertoires of Duse, Bernhardt, and Mrs Patrick Campbell. And she was memorably effective in *The Lady with the Lamp*, a play by Reginald Berkeley about Florence Nightingale, played by Edith Evans, with Gwen as Lady Herbert. In the last two scenes of the play, in which both actresses were required to span many years, Gwen was (as she had in Eve) given a fine opportunity to show her consummate skill in developing her characterisation, and her elderly lady was even better than Edith's.

In 1937 I began to plan a season of four classic plays, to be given, with a permanent company, for runs of six to eight weeks each. Gwen and I were on tour together in a play by

Emlyn Williams, which turned out to be a complete failure in London, when it ran for only twelve performances, but though I had discussed my projected season with Gwen many times in my usually thoughtless way, I proceeded to engage Peggy Ashcroft as my leading lady, and the choice was eagerly seized on in the press. Half way through the season, Michel Saint-Denis agreed to direct the third play *The Three Sisters* of Chekhov, and we both agreed that Gwen would be ideal as the elder sister Olga. When I received from Gwen the only disagreeable letter I ever had from her. I realised how tactlessly I had behaved, and was duly mortified.

Everything, fortunately, was to turn out well. Michel went to see Gwen, who found him fascinating, and his tact and enthusiasm quickly persuaded her to change her mind. She was typically affectionate and forgiving when we started to rehearse, and made immediate and lasting friends with Peggy, while the production turned out to be the biggest success of the whole season.

She continued her immensely varied career in a long series of successful performances, among which I much admired her as the tortured wife in Patrick Hamilton's *Gas Light* and as a stylishly subtle Gwendolen in *The Importance of Being Earnest*. In Graham Greene's *The Potting Shed* she was my mother, and in the Stratford *Lear* she was my daughter Regan, venomous and deadly. In 1942 she played Lady Macbeth with me, a fine performance underrated, I thought, by the critics, who would never accept a small feminine actress in the part until they came to relent at the surprising success of Judi Dench a year or two ago. I had the joy of directing Gwen (Judi was the Anya) in a production of *The Cherry Orchard* at the Lyric, Hammersmith, and thought her Madame Ranevsky finer even than the often brilliant performances of Edith Evans, Peggy Ashcroft and Athene Seyler in different versions of the same play.

I was very sorry to be out of England when she played the drug-taking wife in O'Neill's *Long Day's Journey Into Night*, for many people told me it was the finest performance of her whole career. Today in her nineties, she has remained indefatigably energetic. Though living alone in her Essex cottage, she has lately appeared on television and radio; has given talks at the National and at Stratford; entertains guests at weekends and has made new friends while steeling herself gallantly to the loss of many old ones. Practical, shrewd, philosophical and so greatly talented, she is surely a unique example of a great actress, a generous warm professional colleague, and a most dear and cherished friend.

7

GOLDEN DAYS: THE GUITRYS

It was in the early 1920s that the Guitrys – father and his son Sacha – first appeared in London with their enchanting leading lady, Yvonne Printemps, giving a short season of repertoire under the banner of C. B. Cochran. They were acclaimed by the press and became immediate favourites with the public. Lucien made a tremendous impression with *Pasteur*, a play in which he delivered a long monologue, addressing the theatre audience as if they were students attending a lecture. My parents described this performance to me in some detail, but I was not lucky enough to see it myself.

However I have a most vivid recollection of Lucien's acting in a drama called *Jacqueline*, in which he played an elderly roué who was destined to strangle his mistress in the final scene. It was the preparation for this dénouement in the second act that impressed me most. The scene was a hotel bedroom at Le Touquet where he had taken the girl for a weekend. As Guitry stood over her as she lay on the bed, she suddenly shrank from his embrace crying, 'Oh–! You terrify me.' For a few moments – seconds perhaps – he seemed to grow inches taller and became a towering and sinister creature. Then, suddenly breaking the tension completely, he resumed his normally charming manner for the rest of the scene. I watched him most intently, and am convinced that in fact he did absolutely nothing, moving neither his hands, his face or his body. His absolute stillness and the projection of his concentrated imagination, controlled and executed with consummate technique, produced on the girl and on the audience an extraordinary and unforgettable effect. I knew I had seen a great actor.

Lucien was evidently a tremendous figure both on and off the stage. It was said he could eat twelve dozen snails for supper after a performance. (Fortunate for his stage colleagues that it was not beforehand.) And I once saw a film of contemporary celebrities, including Renoir, Monet and Bernhardt, called *Paris 1900*, compiled by Sacha, which included a fine close-up of Lucien, wearing a big sombrero, with a monocle hanging from the brim on a narrow cord. Both he and his son were great dandies, affecting frilled shirts, fur coats, opera cloaks and elegant walking sticks, obviously proud to be immediately recognisable (even off the stage) as the distinguished personalities they were.

Sacha was enormously talented and prolific, turning out dozens of plays, films and operettas over the years, as well as directing and acting in most of them himself. Yvonne Printemps was said to have been Lucien's *chère amie* at first. Whether this was true or not, she married Sacha not long after his father's death and returned with him many times to London to delight the public with various pieces artfully concocted to display both of them to the best possible advantage.

Yvonne Printemps was a *soubrette*, with a trim, elegant figure, appealing spaniel eyes, and a broad turned-up nose not unlike that of our own Gertrude Lawrence, and her acting had the same inimitable brand of impish sentimental comedy. But unlike Gertie Lawrence, whose singing voice, fascinating as it was, could be distinctly unreliable and wobbly, Printemps' tones were exquisitely delicate and true. She was sometimes tempted, perhaps, to prolong her top notes unduly in order to show off her brilliant breath control, and to yield rather too easily to demands for encores. But in *Mozart* (for which her songs had been composed most skilfully by Reynaldo Hahn) she seemed ravishingly youthful and touching in her powdered wig, black knee breeches and buckled shoes, while Sacha hovered about her with avuncular authority, not attempting to try and sing himself, but contributing a kind of flowing, rhythmic accompaniment with his own speeches, delivered in a deep caressing voice.

In another play with music, *Mariette*, Sacha, as the Emperor Napoleon the Third, sat in a stage box, half hidden by the curtains, his great hands emerging at intervals in their white kid gloves to applaud the heroine as she stood on the stage within a stage; while, in the dressing-room scene that followed, she parried his advances in captivating roulades as he murmured in baffled tones of royal entreaty, 'Venez souper avec moi.'

The gramophone records of Printemps, especially some excerpts from *Les Trois Valses*, which unhappily she never played in London, can still give us a nostalgic memory of her inimitable quality as a singer. But in Noël Coward's *Conversation Piece*, which he wrote specially for her, and which she played with success both in London and New York, she had to learn her part in English, parrot fashion, and was considerably hampered by her difficulty with the language, though her best scene at the climax of the operetta was sung in French.

I was only near her once, when she and Guitry were guests of honour on one of their annual visits, at a dinner dance, given (rather improbably) by the ex-students of the RADA. I timidly ventured towards the high table where she was sitting, beautifully gowned and bejewelled, but Sacha, seated beside her, guessed at my impertinent intention, and growled imperiously, 'Madame ne danse pas', at which I hastily bowed myself away with my tail between my legs.

Sacha was obviously compulsively jealous as a husband, though a notorious ladies' man, and married again several times after Yvonne Printemps finally left him to elope with the actor Pierre Fresnay. But he had evidently taught her to be somewhat possessive herself, since she insisted that Fresnay should never kiss another woman on the stage after she had married him, and he obediently resigned himself to playing saints, priests and confirmed bachelors for the rest of his distinguished career.

I only met Sacha on one occasion. In March 1939 Peggy Ashcroft and I were invited to appear at a gala, to celebrate the state visit of the French President. We were asked to play the balcony scene from *Romeo and Juliet* as part of an entertainment to be given at the Foreign Office in London, the courtyard of which had been covered over and transformed into a theatre for the occasion. It was a tremendous affair, the last of its kind before the war, and I could not help referring to it afterwards as the Duchess of Richmond's Ball. There was a magnificent profusion of flowers edging the balconies, and a positive thicket of madonna lilies dividing the stage from the auditorium.

Before the performance, the guests – glittering with tiaras, long gloves and fans for the women, and uniforms, medals and sashes for the men – distributed themselves on small gilt chairs. Everyone rose as the royal family entered by different doors, Queen Mary from one, the Duke and Duchess of Kent from another, and lastly the King and Queen, who conducted the President and his suite (which included the nefarious Laval) to their armchairs in the front row. We actors dragged ourselves reluctantly away from the peepholes in the curtain and the entertainment began.

It was a long and somewhat patchy programme, as is usual on such occasions. The audience, exhausted by a long day of official functions – a visit to Windsor, the National Gallery, and a state banquet to follow – became increasingly restive in their tight clothes. Several elderly gentlemen seemed to be in some danger of falling asleep and slipping off their chairs, and Peggy Ashcroft and I did not feel that our Shakespeare excerpt was very successful. No doubt we were somewhat inaudible as well, but we were politely received. Edith Evans appeared with a group of distinguished actresses representing the wines of France. But the most strikingly effective moment was the entrance of a band of Scottish pipers, magnificently kilted and bonneted, who swung on to the small stage with a great swirl of bagpipes, marched round it, and swung grandly off again, as everybody woke up and applauded vigorously for the first time.

Sacha Guitry had been invited to appear with Seymour Hicks in a sketch written by them both. Hicks was a great admirer of Sacha and had acted in English versions of several of his plays. The humour of their joint endeavour was supposed to lie in attempts by Sacha to speak English and Hicks to reply in French, but both actors were exceedingly nervous and obviously under-rehearsed. I watched them from the wings as they kept drying up and killing each other's laughs, which were not very plentiful in any case. Appearing with them was Sacha's latest wife, Geneviève Sereville, an extremely young and pretty girl. At the morning rehearsal Peggy and I had been asked to come on to the stage to be introduced to the distinguished visitors. Mademoiselle Sereville was dressed in a very short skirt, and her stockings were rolled below the knees like a footballer's, showing a considerable expanse of bewitching thigh. We stammered a few polite words in our halting French, to which M. Guitry, magnificent with his fur collar and gold-topped cane, made suitably gracious acknowledgment. As we moved away to find our dressing-rooms I ventured to remark to Hicks, 'I say, sir, that's a remarkably attractive girl with M. Guitry don't you think?' and was rewarded by the trenchant comment, 'Try acting with her, old boy. It's the cabman's good-bye.'

8

EMINENT VICTORIANS: SIR SQUIRE BANCROFT, SIR JOHNSTON FORBES-ROBERTSON, DAME MADGE KENDAL

As a young man I often caught a glimpse of two of the great theatrical figures of my parents' time, Sir Squire Bancroft and Sir Johnston Forbes-Robertson. I would pass them as they strolled along Piccadilly in their curly-brimmed top hats and frock coats, the one with wavy white hair and a monocle dangling on a moiré ribbon, the other cadaverous, with sculptured Burne-Jones features. Both men, in their seventies, remained slim, upright, and immensely distinguished.

Of course I never saw either of them on the stage. But I heard glowing praise of 'Forbie' from Leon Quartermaine, who had been an enthusiastic member of his company, and from his daughter Jean, so like him in appearance and so gifted as an actress throughout her brilliant but eventually tragic career. Forbes-Robertson writes in his autobiography that he was only happy in his youth, when he was a painter, and that he left the theatre with intense relief. I was lucky enough on one occasion to hear him give one of the great Hamlet soliloquies in a lecture, and was enormously impressed by his grace and eloquence. A silent film which still exists, though photographed when he was sixty, gives proof of his picturesquely gothic gestures and princely bearing.

Bancroft had retired with a fortune many years before I was born. The number of his productions is surprisingly small, but he revived them many times and they never failed to continue to attract the public. *Diplomacy* (a melodrama adapted from Sardou's *Dora*) was his most notable success. When Bancroft and his wife decided they were too old for the youthful roles they had created, they re-cast them with players of promising young talent and appeared themselves in the older character parts – a very sensible decision. Gerald du Maurier, Owen Nares, and Gladys Cooper appeared in various revivals of the play, which still held the stage as late as the Nineteen Thirties.

When Lady Bancroft, a skilful comedienne in the Marie Tempest manner, died, Sir Squire went to live in Albany. From there he would walk each morning to his bank, when he would demand a slip with the amount of his current balance, which he diligently perused before proceeding to lunch at the Garrick Club. Somewhat morbidly fascinated with mortality, he always visited the bedside of friends who were ill bearing a large bunch of black muscat grapes. He was also a faithful attendant at funerals and memorial services (as well as fashionable theatrical first nights) and was heard to remark, on his return from a cremation service – still something of a novelty in the Twenties – 'A most impressive occasion. And afterwards the relations were kind enough to ask me to go behind.'

But to me the most august figure of the last *monstres sacrés* of the Victorian era was Dame Madge Kendal. I once saw her driving down Shaftesbury Avenue, redfaced and imposing in full evening dress. For some unknown reason her car was lighted up inside, and there she sat, bolt upright, her hair parted in the middle and screwed back into a bun, her neck and shoulders in handsome décolleté. With a sparkling necklace at the throat, and her bodice tightly corseted, with the cleft between her breasts exposed like a portrait by Ingres, she was an awe-inspiring sight.

As a girl she had made her first successes acting at Bristol in a company that included Ellen Terry. Her brother Tom Robertson was the author of *Caste* and other 'cup-and-saucer' plays, as they were called, which inaugurated a completely new series of realistic ensemble productions. Later she married William Kendal, and together they went into management, achieving a hugely successful partnership which rivalled that of the Bancrofts, and the couple were able to retire in early middle age, just as the Bancrofts did, with comfortable bank accounts and legendary reputations.

Many people, including my father and James Agate, considered Mrs Kendal the finest actress in England, a mistress of comedy and domestic drama even surpassing Ellen Terry. She seldom ventured into the classic field, however, and the photographs of her as Rosalind/Ganymede – with Kendal as Orlando sporting a resplendent Victorian moustache – suggest a rather over-corseted, buskinned Amazon. But she triumphed in Tree's famous *The Merry Wives of Windsor* for the Coronation of Edward the Seventh in 1902, when she and Ellen Terry shared the honours with him, though Mrs Kendal had always disapproved of Ellen's divorces, love affairs and illegitimate children. Tree hid in a box to watch their reunion at the first rehearsal, chuckling with glee at expected tantrums, but the ladies seem to have behaved to one another with admirable restraint. The subsequent publicity and box-office returns did much, no doubt, to sweeten their differences, though I noticed that in the revival of the same production the following year, Mrs Kendal did not appear.

On her eightieth birthday Dame Madge (as she was by now) being asked to record a speech for broadcasting, chose to read the epilogue from *As You Like It*. Arriving at the BBC she was received with respectful ceremony. The director showed her where to stand and pointing to the microphone explained politely 'and that, Dame Madge, is your Orlando'. To which the old lady replied with a gracious smile, 'Ah, my husband was better looking than that.'

Her autobiography is sadly disappointing reading, showing her to have been a tremendous snob, and full of self-pity about her children's treatment of her. She even refers to herself as Mater Dolorosa, though actually she herself had treated them very cruelly. But evidently she was a brilliant and professional artist, a fine director and trainer of young talents (Marie Löhr and Mary Jerrold both spoke of her with affection and respect) and in her last years she was an amusing and impressive personality, speaking at public dinners (I once heard her imitate Phelps playing Macbeth) and making appeals at charity matinées. Having been shown the box where she was later to be received by royalty, prior to one of these occasions, she announced, 'I must go down to the stage for a moment. I haven't felt my roof.' And descending to the footlights she gazed towards the gallery, where the cleaners were working busily, and called out in silvery tones, 'Ladies, can you hear me?'

She wrote several amusing letters to the newspapers deploring the behaviour of the Bright Young Things, and castigating the new fashions – cigarette smoking, short skirts, lipsticks, and making-up in public. To the end of her life – as one can see in Orpen's splendid portrait of her in the National Portrait Gallery – she always wore Victorian bonnets decked with flowers and tied under her chin.

When I was playing Benedick at Sadler's Wells in 1930, Dorothy Green and I were summoned to her box during an interval, where she greeted (and shortly afterwards dismissed us) as if she were royalty, with a few patronisingly gracious remarks. But Seymour Hicks tells a tragic story of his last meeting with her. Mortally ill, she sent him an urgent message, and he arrived at her house in Portland Place and was shown in to an empty room with all the blinds drawn. Dame Madge rushed in a few moments later, haggard and dishevelled in a dressing gown, and fell to her knees, exclaiming, 'I have wronged my children. I am a wicked woman.' Mater Dolorosa indeed.

Quite recently she was depicted as a character in a new play, and afterwards a film, *The Elephant Man*, about a poor deformed creature whose horrific appearance created great publicity at the turn of the century. It seems that Mrs Kendal visited and befriended him, as did also Queen Alexandra. Two of the film critics referred to the character playing the visiting lady – one as 'Mrs Kendall', the other as 'Mrs Kemble' (could they have mixed her up with Sarah Siddons perhaps?). Such is the ephemeral nature of theatrical memories. Dame Madge would not have been amused.

In the film she was played with considerable glamour by the American film star Anne Bancroft, but I thought a great effect had been missed by not depicting the severe, buttoned-up dignity of the original actress, for whom the episode must have been a most painful and rather courageous experience, but also showed there must have been a compassionate streak in her apparently rigid nature.

28th January 1978

9

AUNT MABEL TERRY-LEWIS

My Aunt Mabel was the youngest of my mother's three sisters. She was also the prettiest and the most elegant. Somewhat sharp-tongued and opinionated, she darted in and out of my parents' house when we were children, and at my grandmother's house there was a full-length portrait of her by John Collier that I much admired in which she was sitting in an imposing chair, dressed in a long black velvet teagown.

As a boy I was particularly fascinated by her because I knew she had formerly been an actress. But when I first knew her as a boy she had been married for several years and given up the stage to live in the country with her husband, a captain of Territorials and, presumably, well-to-do. They had no children. My father told me that Mabel had once been engaged to his own brother, but he had evidently found her somewhat too demanding. On one occasion, when he was to escort her to a ball, she had sent him back half-way across London to retrieve the gloves which she had left at home.

She had made her stage début in the Nineties, when her mother (my grandmother Kate Terry) had emerged, after many years' retirement, to help launch her daughter in a long-forgotten piece called *The Master* with Sir John Hare. The play only lasted a few weeks, but Mabel's talent was immediately recognised, and she appeared subsequently in a number of good *ingénue* parts, among them the young girl in Pinero's *Gay Lord Quex*. But I was surprised to find that her attitude towards the theatre was curiously patronising. She told me once that she had been in love with Guy du Maurier, the author of a well-known War play, called *An Englishman's*

Home. 'But what about his brother, Gerald?' I enquired,
'weren't you in love with him too?' 'In love?' replied Mabel
sharply, 'with an *actor*?'

She and her husband lived in Dorsetshire, and when I was
in my early teens they invited me down to stay with them.
There were white doves on the lawn, a dairy where I licked
cream off my greedy fingers from the open bowls, and
delicious meals. But I was absurdly homesick and dismayed
by the quiet of the country where I had seldom been except
on family holidays. I can remember sitting in the downstairs
lavatory gazing ruefully at a decorative plaque over the washstand which announced in raised capital letters EAST OR WEST,
HOME IS BEST.

But I liked helping to pick mushrooms in the wet fields
and bringing them back to eat for breakfast, almost as much
as I disliked accompanying Mabel's husband, when he went
out shooting, attended by several spaniels – one of them with
a raw wound on its back which glittered repulsively in the
sunshine.

In the evening, however, Mabel would descend in a becoming teagown and lie on the sofa with her feet up. Reassured
by her charm, I became more than ever convinced that the
theatre must somehow be the career I was determined to
pursue. To my great delight my aunt decided to stage a series
of performances of a one-act play by Gertrude Jennings called
The Bathroom Door, considered at that time, I suppose, the
least bit daring, since all the characters appeared in dressing-
gowns, night-gowns and pyjamas. In this I was to play the
juvenile and Mabel herself the Prima Donna (the leading lady
naturally), and we acted in village halls for the benefit of the
local Women's Institute where it was all a great success.

Mabel was something of a snob. She loved titled folk and
Royalty. Lord Ilchester was one of her neighbours and she
was very much the Lady of the Manor, patronising bazaars
and point-to-point meetings and giving bridge and tennis
parties. But when, after the first War, her husband died,
she suddenly decided to employ her boundless energies by
returning to the stage. It may be that she needed money too.

She re-appeared in a political comedy by H. M. Harwood,
called *A Grain of Mustard Seed* in the early Twenties and made
an immediate personal success. Her style and technique were

quite unimpaired by her long absence from the theatre. Her carriage and diction were always faultless, and she continued to act for twenty years, both in London and New York, in a succession of aristocratic roles which fitted her to perfection. She was quite without humour and amazingly self-contained. She demanded (and obtained) permission to be absent from the cast at a matinée in a du Maurier revival of *Dear Brutus* because she had arranged to go to the Derby. She also insisted on driving a very shabby car with several spaniels on her lap and an array of rubber sponges lashed to the wheel to counter her rheumatism.

I doubt if she ever read a book. When she played Lady Bracknell in *The Importance of Being Ernest* with me at the Lyric, Hammersmith in 1929, she had no idea that her lines were funny. 'What on earth are they laughing at?' she used to say. And since, with a rather shaky memory, she would frequently have to be prompted by one or other of us in the cast, we were further dismayed to discover that, during the second act, in which Lady Bracknell does not appear, Mabel had lain down amongst the spaniels on the floor in her dressing-room and enjoyed an hour's nap, returning for the final scene more vague and absentminded than ever. Nevertheless, she made a great success of the part, which she played with her usual grace and distinction, and only the definitive creation achieved by Edith Evans in the 1939 production eclipsed her performance completely, which must have been somewhat galling to her vanity, though she was far too dignified ever to mention it to me.

Unhappily, her last engagement led to a very embarrassing situation. Hugh Beaumont engaged her to play the Duchess of Berwick in a 1946 revival of *Lady Windermere's Fan*, which was to open in Manchester for a short provincial tour before coming to the Haymarket Theatre, and I was asked to direct the play. At rehearsal, Mabel was quite unsure of her lines and made endless pauses and mistakes, even calling characters by the wrong names, which was somewhat confusing to the plot. She crossed swords with Cecil Beaton over her costumes, which she thought over-showy and unbecoming, and thwarted all my attempts to persuade her to rehearse and memorise correctly, spending her days on tour motoring about to look at houses and visit friends. This resulted in her

giving a more confused performance than ever, though her
elegant period manner and grace of movement won her a
round of applause on her exit almost every night.

Finally we decided we had no choice but to replace her,
and Beaumont agreed to go to Leeds and break the news, a
mission which I was too cowardly to undertake myself but
which I am sure he carried out with great reluctance and
considerable tact. It was an extremely sad ending to a distinguished career, and I was ashamed to be involved in it,
only telling myself that the theatre had never meant anything
deeply serious to my aunt. All her life she had scattered her
talents and interests in too many directions. She painted
miniatures and was an expert needlewoman. Her houses
and gardens were somewhat ramshackle but always cosy,
attractive and charmingly arranged. She inspired great devotion in the servants and companions who ministered to her
with such affectionate attention, and was always kind and
amusing in a superficial way. But I found it sad that her
professional efficiency and inherited instinct for the stage
never seemed to fire her ambitions and allow her to take her
work more seriously.

10

ANNIE ESMOND: THE OLD CHARACTER ACTRESS

In the last year of the war I was acting every night and rehearsing during the day, so I was very reluctant to comply when the secretary of the management for whom I was working suddenly telephoned me, saying, 'You ought to go and see Annie Esmond. She wants to see you, and I think she is dying.' With my usual dread of hospitals and nursing-homes, I finally braced myself to the ordeal, and have been thankful ever since that I did so, although the poor old lady was the colour of mahogany, gasping for breath, and obviously drugged and desperate, only able to mumble a few almost incoherent words. I sat at her bedside for twenty minutes, while she held my hand tightly and gazed at me beseechingly. Later that day I was told that she had died.

I had never known her except when I worked with her in the theatre, though before I became a professional actor, when I used to see every play I could, I had admired her acting in a number of plays in the West End, supporting famous stars such as Charles Hawtrey and Lilian Braithwaite. She was unusually tall for a woman, with a somewhat formidably grim appearance but a charming smile. I met her first, for a couple of special performances for the Stage Society, in an early O'Neill play called *The Great God Brown* in which she played my mother, and we all carried masks which we assumed at intervals throughout the play – a rather pretentious and unsatisfactory affair, it seemed to me.

She confided to me at that time that she had a tremendous

admiration and affection for two leading players of the period, Leslie Faber and Yvonne Arnaud, both of whom I also greatly admired, and of course I was much impressed to share her enthusiasm for them both. We did not meet again until 1938, when we were both engaged to appear with Dame Marie Tempest in Dodie Smith's *Dear Octopus*. Annie played the children's Nanny in the large cast of this family play, which, though it opened on the night of Munich, had an enormous success with the public and ran for more than a year – but I hardly remember talking to her, as we had no scenes together and so many other people were involved. I left the play when the war broke out, and did not see her again until 1942, when I was planning a production of *Macbeth*, which I was to direct and appear in for a long provincial tour before bringing it to London.

I suggested Annie Esmond for the Second Witch, and she immediately agreed to accept the part, even though the designer, Michael Ayrton, had created for the character a grotesque headdress of stag's antlers surmounting bare legs and ugly rags. The rehearsals, held in the draughty wastes of the Scala Theatre in Charlotte Street (long pulled down) were infinitely depressing in winter weather. We tried to make the best of it, and christened Annie 'Sitting Bull' as she squatted beside the witches' cauldron, and we laboured for hours trying to synchronise the rhyming lines of her few scenes to the recorded background of William Walton's music.

The usual disasters of tradition occurred during the tour, when two of the cast died, and there were replacements, accidents, and other complications. Someone told me that Annie had trudged round Glasgow trying to find cheaper digs. I gave her lunch occasionally and became as fond of her as ever, and I was very glad to be able to insist, when the production eventually opened in London, that she should have rather more important billing and a less inconvenient dressing-room, as she well deserved. In the following year, after I had played in and directed a revival of Barrie's *Dear Brutus* in London, I took the production to several military camps to play it to the troops. Mary Jerrold, an enchanting Barrie actress, had to leave the cast owing to her husband's sudden death, and Annie readily agreed to replace her.

One afternoon, when we were acting at Cheltenham, she suddenly surprised me by asking to see me in private. She produced the official form which had to be filled in before setting off on the ENSA tour and burst into tears. 'What can I put down?' she sobbed. 'I have never known who my father was.' I tried to calm her, assuring her that her stage name would surely be accepted without question, but realising of course that she had been evidently ashamed of her illegitimacy all her life and had probably never confessed it to anyone before.

In 1944 I gave a season of four plays in repertory at the Haymarket Theatre, but, when Annie came to see me begging for a part, however small, I was very sorry to have to admit that there was nothing I could offer her. The air-raids and buzz-bombs were still a continual menace, and Annie, who lived alone, wore a whistle round her neck for fear she might be buried alive. Finally I suggested apologetically that she might care to walk-on in *Hamlet*, play a part (of one scene) in *Love for Love* as the Nurse, and understudy her adored Yvonne Arnaud in Maugham's *The Circle*, and she agreed immediately, glad to be relieved of the loneliness which coming to the theatre and mixing with the company would remove.

She must have been already ill that year, for at the dress rehearsal of *The Circle* in Edinburgh she suddenly rushed on to the stage, snatched the hat from Yvonne Arnaud's head, and cried out, 'I have no costumes provided for me in case I ever have to go on.' The matter was quickly seen to, and we opened the play in London, but after a few nights I was told that Annie had been suddenly taken ill, and she never appeared in the theatre again.

Some months after her death, I received a solicitor's letter telling me she had left me £5,000 in her will, the exact amount I needed to pay for the premium on a house I had just taken in Westminster, where I was to live for the next thirty years. There was an equal sum left to Edna May (the star of the famous Edwardian musical comedy about the Salvation Army), and a number of smaller bequests to various friends which were able to be increased, since her estate amounted to £15,000. Yet she had lived alone for years in a single room. I never opened my front door in Cowley Street without thinking of her touching generosity and her professional dedication to her work.

11

THE WIGMAKER

Willie Clarkson was a somewhat preposterous Dickensian figure, part Fagin, part Quilp, with a dash of Mr Mantalini. As he entered a theatre on a fashionable first night he would be greeted by a slight flutter of applause from the occupants of the pit and gallery, though their warmest outbursts were reserved for the theatrical celebrities of the day – the leading ladies and actor-managers – who timed their entrances so discreetly and turned towards the cheaper parts of the house to bow their acknowledgments as they took their seats.

Willie was short and plump. Beneath his black satin stock his chest protruded like a pouter pigeon's, decked in an elaborately frilled shirt with diamond studs over a brocaded waistcoat. His waist was tightly corseted and his stumpy bow legs ended in tiny feet encased in glossy high-heeled boots. He wore white kid gloves with black stitchings on the back of them and carried ivory opera glasses on a long gold handle. His red hair, curly moustaches, and full Edwardian beard, were dyed and crimped, his face patently rouged and powdered, and as he bustled in, waving his opera hat in all directions, he nodded and lisped greetings to the people sitting round him in the stalls.

I saw him again one night at the Chelsea Arts Ball, an annual jamboree held at the Albert Hall every New Year's Eve, where everyone wore fancy dress, and the night's revels usually ended in something of an orgy. Clarkson appeared leading the procession which paraded round the Hall just before midnight. He was dressed as a Sultan, with wide silk trousers tied with a huge sash, and curly-toed slippers. On his head was an enormous turban, in the front of which a tall aigrette was fastened by a gigantic property jewel. He was attended by a cortège of extremely unattractive ladies (probably assistants at his emporium in the daytime), clad in gauzy veils and yashmaks, and clattering with beads and bracelets. Willie marched round the Hall in front of the group, brandishing a long ebony stick with a cluster of false diamonds attached to the top of it, grinning and gesticulating like the Demon King.

I have no idea how old he must have been when I was first aware of him, but he was *the* theatrical wigmaker right up to the 1920s, when Madame Gustave, who soon after this time opened a rival wig shop in Covent Garden, began to surpass him with more modern merchandise and greater efficiency of workmanship, losing him a number of his former customers.

Clarkson was already famous right back in the Nineties, when Queen Victoria, after so many years of complete retirement, began in her old age to encourage private theatricals and tableaux vivants performed by her children and courtiers when she was at Windsor. She even commanded professional companies (Irving and Ellen Terry, the Kendals, the Bancrofts, and others), to mount miniature copies of their London successes and appear before her in the Waterloo Chamber at the Castle, thereby greatly increasing their professional reputations.

Russell Thorndike told me a fantastic (and I fear quite apocryphal) story of an afternoon when, as an apprentice choirboy to the Chapel at Windsor, he was told to go down to the station to meet Clarkson, who was due to arrive with his wigs, costumes, and make-up boxes to supervise one of the fashionable private performances. According to Russell, Willie was suddenly taken short as he puffed up the steep incline to the Castle. Fortunately Russell was able to direct him hastily to a small lavatory nearby and Clarkson dashed inside. At this very moment, a bathchair, with the Queen herself sitting in it, attended by the Munshi, her Indian servant, was seen descending the slope in the direction of the convenience. Russell hissed through the keyhole, 'The Queen is coming. It's the Queen.' On which a voice came lisping through the locked door, 'It'th all right, your Majesty. Only old Willie Clarkson thitting on his own inithials!'

There is another similar story told of him at Windsor. (Lavatory jokes were evidently popular at the turn of the century.) 'I was just going along a passage in the Castle,' Willie said, 'when who should I thpy but Her Majesty herself coming out of a thertain apartment!' 'What on earth did you do, Willie?' 'Oh, I jutht murmured, "Honi thoit qui mal y penthe, Your Majesty" and thwept on!'

Under Royal Patronage, of course, Willie's fame and fortune grew and prospered. He created wigs for Sarah Bernhardt, and even flew over to Paris in one of the early aeroplanes to attend one of her dress rehearsals. She opened his shop in Wardour Street (long since demolished and rebuilt) where the plaque she unveiled to celebrate the event could still be seen till quite recently on one of the pillars of the portico. As a student at Drama School, and for several years after I became a professional actor, I would go to the shop to hire wigs or buy grease-paints (sticks of Leichner were what we used in those days). Clarkson also sold the big oblong tinned japanned make-up boxes with flexible shelves and compartments which many actors then used in their dressing-rooms. When I went on tour for the first time, my parents gave me one as a present and of course I was immensely proud of it.

Clarkson's shop was rather spooky; poorly lit, with stained-glass windows on the steep stairs to the first floor, dusty and cluttered with suits of armour, weapons, play bills, masks – a positive Aladdin's Cave of theatrical paraphernalia, and the walls covered with signed photographs of Willie's most famous clients, presented to him with flattering dedications. Clarkson lurked in the recesses of the shop, but nearly always darted out when he heard the bell which rang as the front door was opened. He would sometimes proffer free theatre tickets, as well as a stream of snobbish reminiscence and encouragement, to young male customers, and we always took care to avoid getting too close to him, in case his hands should become unduly familiar or a visit to his private sanctum be proposed, though I never heard of him actually making a pass at anyone. The best one could hope for would be that youthful looks might be a passport to a rather better wig, since the stock ones usually provided for the hoi polloi were inclined to be shabby, much worn, and unattractive both in quality and in appearance.

Stage wigs in those days nearly always had forehead pieces
of pink linen which had to be joined cunningly with grease
paint to the make-up on the rest of one's face, a difficult and
often unconvincing process, especially for young beginners.
The foundation of the wig was thick and one sweated pro-
fusely in hot weather. In the last fifty years, of course, the
whole art of wigmaking (like that of theatre and film make-up
as well) has been completely modernised, and today wigs are
very light and easy to wear as well as being completely
convincing from the audience. But even as late as 1931, Noël
Coward came to see *Musical Chairs*, a play in which Frank
Vosper was playing my father. When the curtain rose on the
second act I was dismayed to observe that he had disappeared.
Meeting him a few weeks later, he apologised, remarking, as
he wagged a reproving finger, 'Couldn't bear to stay. You
were overacting so disgracefully, and Vosper's wig looked
like a yachting-cap!'

Clarkson was reputed to be extremely disreputable and
extremely rich. His star clients were attended by his head
assistant, Mr Sussex, a gloomy-looking, elderly man with a
huge Kitchener moustache and a long white apron, but we
small fry were not considered of sufficient importance to be
candidates for his ministrations.

Willie's end was sudden and dramatic. He became somewhat involved in a blackmail case. Then a fire broke out on
his premises which no one seemed to be able to account for,
and soon afterwards he was found dead in bed in his flat above
the shop. I have no idea whether he left a fortune or whom
he could have bequeathed it to if he did.

I have always thought what an effective central character
he would make in some lurid thriller, for he was certainly an
amusing old rip – a mysterious, highly coloured eccentric of
the deepest dye.

12

THE TEA CEREMONY AND
THE SITWELLS

I have always been astonished at the English passion for drinking tea, a beverage that I have never found essential to my own well-being. Yet almost everyone I know seems to demand it at regular intervals throughout the day, beginning with a cup brought to them by some willing hand, if possible, before they even rise from bed. There are compulsory tea-breaks in factories, rehearsal studios, building-sites and offices, yet I cannot but resent the ever-present recommendations of a 'cuppa' which greet me on hoardings and try to woo me in television commercials. I was once dismayed to find so fastidious a writer as the late Somerset Maugham, remarking (in his determination to be an adept observer of up-to-date colloquial slang) in one of his later novels that a character is 'not his cup of tea'.

However, I have to admit that in my own boyhood and adolescence, when tea was an established meal as well as merely something to drink, I looked forward to indulging in its more solid adjuncts with unmitigated greed. Nursery tea – strong and Indian, with rock cakes, (buns and crumpets in wintertime), china and dainty sandwiches for the grown-ups. Teashop outings with my mother, at the Devonshire Dairies, opposite Selfridge's in Oxford Street, with clotted cream, scones, and raspberry jam. High teas on holidays in the country – shrimps, hard-boiled eggs, salad and cold meat. Rich teas at Gunter's – ices slightly flavoured with salt. Elaborate teas at Rumpelmayers, where one walked up the length of the room to a platform where an array of cakes were spread out on tables, and one stood choosing greedily, plate in one hand, fork in the other, and returned with a heap of richness piled up, nervously glancing to right and left and hoping the other customers were not taking too much notice. Even Maison Lyons in those days could proffer varied, though somewhat less patrician, confections – ice cream sodas, knickerbocker glories and banana splits. An actor friend of mine, lured there after a matinée by an adoring fan, was momentarily taken aback when she politely enquired: 'Do you prefer cake or gâteau?'

I don't think my parents ever drank tea at all themselves, though of course they provided it for guests, but my eldest brother, who was somewhat fastidious in his tastes, taught me to like very weak China tea with a slice of lemon, though I always felt somewhat shy at asking for it away from home. Badly wounded in the First War, he used to beg the orderlies in the hospital not to give him the strong Indian brew which everybody else appeared to relish, and they would stare at him in bewilderment and say, 'Don't you even like to taste the tea, sir?'

The Victorians and Edwardians, of course, considered afternoon tea an established fixture in their daily curriculum of gargantuan repasts, and their tables groaned with an elaborate paraphernalia of kettles, silver, cakestands, spirit-lamps, tea caddies, doilies, lace table-cloths and rich displays of food.

Two tea parties have always been among my cherished memories. I was playing Hamlet in 1944 at the beautiful Haymarket Theatre, where my dressing-room – where I sometimes fire-watched also – was on the top floor up a long flight of shallow stairs. (In winter there was even a coal fire in the grate, a privilege long since abandoned.) One evening an elderly lady climbed those stairs at the end of the performance. Her name was Mrs Carnegie, and she was certainly in her eighties. I immediately recognised her as the wife of Canon Carnegie, whom I had once seen, when I was still a boarder at Westminster School during the Great War, sitting with her family in the Norman undercroft in the Abbey cloisters. Her husband, magnificently tall and distinguished, was also part of the group, and they shared the shelter with

other clerics and their families as well as some twenty of us
schoolboys, all of whom were ordered to leave our dormitor-
ies in Dean's Yard and to take refuge there whenever the
zeppelin raids occurred. We would occasionally dash into the
cloisters to watch the searchlights and the flash of gunfire
over the Abbey roofs, though, of course, such rashness was
discouraged by the master in charge of us.

Now, so many years later, I ventured to remind my visitor
of this episode as she congratulated me on my acting, and she
promptly invited me to call on her for tea the following day.
Her house in Egerton Crescent was elegant and beautifully
kept. An elderly butler ushered me into a drawing-room full
of presentation scrolls and caskets (I realised by this time
that Mrs Carnegie had formerly been the wife of Joseph
Chamberlain, the eminent Birmingham politician and father
of Austen and Neville), and above the fireplace was a striking
portrait of my hostess which appeared to be (and probably
was) by Sargent. The only concessions to wartime conditions
were evident in the white linen loose covers which shrouded
the chairs and sofas.

A large tray was brought in, and Mrs Carnegie, talking
busily all the while of her American grandchildren, whom
she hopefully expected to spend the coming Christmas with
her, proceeded to warm the cups with hot water, from the
silver kettle, before mixing different blends of tea from silver
caddies. There were hot scones under a covered dish, sandwiches and cakes. I sat entranced.

It so happened that I was rehearsing at the time a revival
of Wilde's *Lady Windermere's Fan*, which I had been engaged
to direct, and the scene in the first act, when the heroine has to
play a flirtatious exchange at the tea-table with her would-be
seducer, was proving very difficult to bring to life. I told the
young actress playing Lady W. of my visit to Mrs Carnegie's,
and begged her to introduce the detail I had observed with
such fascination. But, alas, she refused to be fired by my
enthusiasm. 'Oh no,' she cried. 'I could never manage it – all
those bits and pieces to handle and manipulate as well as
timing that complicated dialogue!' But I still hope to see the
tea ceremony correctly reproduced on the stage in some
Victorian or Edwardian revival.

My second tea party was to take place, many years later,

John Gielgud as a boy

Ellen Terry as Queen Katharine and Edith Craig as her lady-in-waiting in *Henry VIII* at the Lyceum Theatre, 1892

Fred Terry.

Marion Terry with A.E. Matthews in *Peter's Mother* at Wyndham's Theatre, 1906

John Gielgud and Mabel Terry–
Lewis in *The Importance of Being
Earnest* at The Lyric,
Hammersmith, 1929

Edward Gordon Craig, 1956

Lilian Braithwaite and Gerald du Maurier in *Nobody's Daughter*

Madge Titheradge in *A Doll's House*, November 1925

when I was acting in New York. I had been given an introduction to Mrs Murray Crane, a wealthy elderly lady with a spacious and beautiful apartment on Fifth Avenue, and she too invited me to tea, when she entertained me with similar elaborate trappings – menservants, silver, covered dishes and exquisite china. Most of the male guests were officials from museums and galleries, and the occasion was crowned by the presence of two legendary ladies, Dame Edith Sitwell and Baroness Karen Blixen-Finecke.

I had first met Dame Edith at luncheon in London (at the house of Sibyl Colefax, the famous lion-hunter) and had been amused and surprised to find her so congenial, as she talked freely – and somewhat slyly – about her own taste in clothes and jewellery.

THE SITWELLS

It was during the early Twenties, when I was acting at Oxford, an earnest beginner and a member of J. B. Fagan's Repertory Company at the Playhouse (which included Flora Robson and Tyrone Guthrie among its members), that I had first become aware of Edith Sitwell.

I had recently made the acquaintance of a number of undergraduates of my own age who were then making their mark in the aesthetic circles of the University. Among them were Evelyn Waugh, Robert Byron, the notoriously decadent Brian Howard, and Harold Acton, who is exactly the same age as I am. The latter always delighted me by his meticulous pronunciation and elegant deportment. He would usually carry a walking-stick, and would bow courteously as we passed each other in the street. It was he who described to me a recent visit of the poetess Edith Sitwell to lunch with him in his rooms, where an intimate circle of his friends had gathered to receive her, and who rose politely as she appeared in the doorway, looking, he said, like Edward the Second in the last act of Marlowe's play, with her long green gown splashed and muddied from the puddles in the Quad, while Harold, advancing with outstretched hands murmured, 'Ah, dear Edith, welcome to our unhappy Gothic midst.'

In those far-off days I was sublimely ignorant of the many-sided talents of the Sitwell family. Not long afterwards, sitting in the pit of the Duke of York's Theatre, I laughed uproariously at one of the most successful items in Noël Coward's first revue *London Calling*. Coward had written all the songs and scenes himself, and he acted, sang and danced as well. (He had been coached by the great Fred Astaire, and was partnered by the brilliant Gertrude Lawrence.) I was greatly impressed by his all round versatility, little thinking that a year or two later I should have the luck to understudy him in his first big dramatic success *The Vortex*.

In the skit which was a feature of the revue, two brothers, Gob and Knob, performed on weirdly sounding musical instruments, dressed in velvet jackets and check trousers, accompanying their sister Hernia Whittlebot (in the person of the splendid matronly comedienne Maisie Gay) as she spouted a series of preposterous verses, swathed in purple draperies, with a wreath of grapes and vine leaves tipped roguishly over one eye.

I was not aware until long afterwards how deeply the Sitwells had resented this unmannerly caricature of their recent controversial recital of *Façade*. Indeed, it was not until Coward wrote a letter to Edith Sitwell not long before her death that a reconciliation was achieved, followed by a tea party at her flat during which they gracefully agreed to bury the hatchet.

In my extreme youth I had the pleasure of meeting Osbert and Sacheverell at a supper party in a studio near Bond Street, and was dazzled by the brilliant conversational power and generosity which they extended to me, a complete stranger. I remember thinking, when I returned home that night, that the talk of Wilde and Alfred Douglas, Robert Ross, and Reggie Turner, must have had that kind of sparkle and repartee, and I regret that I never wrote any of it down to remind me of the subjects that were discussed during that evening, which I have always remembered with delight. How rare it is to sit at a table with really witty and generous guests, who can shine so spontaneously and rivet one's interest without making one feel totally inadequate oneself.

All three Sitwells, if they happened to like you (but of course they could be very cantankerous if they didn't!) always struck me as superb conversationalists. The Russian painter,

Pavel Tchelitchew (a great friend of Edith Sitwell's, with whom he enjoyed a long and stormy friendship and who I met in New York long afterwards in 1936) had also an amazing descriptive talent as a talker, and I remember an afternoon in his studio when he not only described in detail his mother's wedding dress, but also a performance which he had attended in his youth, at the Opera in St Petersburg, when the prima ballerina, smothered in real jewellery, danced on point on the sloping deck of a sinking ship.

But it was not until, just before the Second World War, that I sat next to Edith Sitwell at one of Lady Colefax's fascinating lunch parties in Lord North Street, and was amazed to find her so human and agreeable. She even made fun of the immense rings and necklaces she was wearing that day, and immediately charmed me with her beautiful manners. Some years later she dedicated a poem to me, sending me the original in her own handwriting – a highly surrealist piece which I could not pretend to understand, much as I appreciated the implied compliment.

As I began to meet her more often, she would sometimes write me amusingly characteristic letters about plays in which she had seen me act, and in 1955, when I was playing King Lear in a very abstract and avant-garde production, she came round to my dressing-room after the performance and discussed the play with me at some length. Once or twice she invited me to luncheons at the Sesame Club in Brook Street, where I sat amongst poets and literary lions whom she delighted to entertain there from time to time.

The lady members at the other tables would sink into hushed silence as we trooped in behind our hostess, splendidly gowned and turbanned, with huge aquamarines displayed on her beautiful hands. At the end of one of these occasions we were ushered upstairs to listen to Mrs Gordon Woodhouse playing Bach and Couperin on her clavichord, though only those close enough to the instrument could hear the tinkling music properly against the competition of the traffic roaring past outside.

One year when I was acting in New York, I called on Dame Edith at the St Regis Hotel. She and her brother Osbert were engaged on one of their poetry-reading tours, and were being duly lionised by New York literary society. Edith seemed to me touchingly out of place in the conventional grandeur of her hotel suite, and I found her struggling with a very dull lady visitor (perhaps a distant relation or merely an ardent fan) and admired her patience as she sat bolt upright, tolerating her guest, who kept up a flow of flattering platitudes punctuated by embarrassed pauses. She seemed very pleased to be interrupted by my arrival, and invited me to a preview of a reading of *Macbeth*, which had been arranged to be given in her honour at the Museum of Modern Art at eleven thirty a few mornings later.

This was a very strange, and not very happy, occasion, though it had its amusing side, though less so perhaps to its participants.

The cinema hall in the basement of the museum had been arranged for the recital, with two imposing desks on the raised platform. Edith made a most impressive entrance through the auditorium and received a great ovation from the fashionable audience. She wore a turban and a huge enveloping robe of figured brocade, looking like a spinster Pope as she took up her position in sole possession of one of the desks. Several feet away she was flanked by Glenway Westcott, who was to read the part of Macbeth, and wore a dinner jacket, with a discreet gold neck chain peeping beneath the collar of his frilled shirt – and the third member of the company (who shared his desk), was a fluffy-looking lady in evening dress with flowing skirts, who was to read the part of Lady Macbeth's Gentlewoman and any other odd lines required to give necessary cues to the two principal performers. The reading started very shakily. Edith muddled her pages and fumbled with her spectacles before announcing in ringing tones: 'Act three, scene two – *No*, Act *two*, scene *one*.' Her reading of the verse was sensitive and meticulous, but curiously lacking in dramatic power, and the whole performance seemed to me sadly incongruous and ill-advised.

At the celebration of her seventy-fifth birthday there was a great gathering at the Festival Hall. Edith was brought on to the stage, now sadly enthroned in a wheel chair, wearing a golden gown and a round golden hat, worn like a halo high above her noble forehead. She raised her arms in a wild kind of Papal blessing in acknowledgment of the applause that greeted her appearance, but the microphone attached to the front of her dress slipped out of place almost as soon as she began to speak, and little of her reading was audible in the big auditorium. After the performance, in which *Façade* was read by Sebastian Shaw and Irene Worth, and pieces by William Walton played by the orchestra, she proceeded to give a huge dinner party in the restaurant upstairs.

I had hoped to be able to slip away, but finding I had been allotted a place at Edith's own table, did not like to seem discourteous, and found myself sitting next to Edith's nurse, who delighted me by telling me what a splendid and courageous patient she had the privilege of tending.

After her death, when Osbert began to suffer from his long and protracted struggle against Parkinson's Disease, he remained gallant and determined as ever. I used to have my hair cut at Trumpers in Curzon Street in those days, and Osbert would always greet me and his barber and chat to us both with the greatest liveliness and good humour, though he could hardly walk and trembled violently all the time he was being shaved. He even invited me to supper one evening at Carlyle Square, and insisted on getting up from the table several times to pour wine and serve the food with infinite tact and care.

My final memory of him was at Brighton, just before he was to leave England for the last time. We were both staying at the Metropole Hotel, and every morning he would sit in his wheel chair in the hall, beautifully shaved and tidy. Twice he asked me to have lunch with him, but these were agonising occasions, as he could not help spilling his food, and his voice would suddenly fail him soon after he had begun an anecdote, making it very difficult to know how to answer.

I was acting at the Theatre Royal, Brighton in Chekhov's *Ivanov* and Osbert's male nurse told me one day that he would like to come to a performance. Of course I arranged aisle seats at the end of the row, to enable him to manipulate his chair, and at the end of the play I received a message asking me to go to speak to them in the stalls. As I came into the empty auditorium, there they were, he and his male nurse, sitting waiting for me, both dressed in dinner jackets, a superb touch of courtesy which moved me very much – 'The Grand Manner' as my father used to say.

13

LADY BOUNTIFUL

I could hardly fail to notice her as she sat, several times a week, in the middle of the front row of the stalls at the New Theatre where I was acting in *Richard of Bordeaux*. Sometimes she came alone, sometimes with parties of friends, always elegantly dressed in black lace or white satin. Soon I began to receive charming notes of appreciation which I would answer in suitably polite acknowledgment, and finally I invited her to visit me in my dressing-room.

She was then I suppose in her late sixties, imposing, dignified and motherly, with a charming pussycat smile and a golden plait binding her white hair like a tiara, and her head was apt to shake a little as she talked with great enthusiasm and vitality.

Lavish presents began to arrive at my flat several times a week – fruit, flowers and books in expensive bindings. Soon she invited me to lunch at her beautiful house in Charles Street, where the banisters were curved outwards to allow easy passage to hooped skirts and crinolines, and there were menservants and elaborate meals beautifully served. She told me she had once lived in Berkeley Square, and had given a cotillion party for the then Prince of Wales, for which she had arranged that two flower shops should remain open all night to provide fresh bouquets and buttonholes for the guests. She was incorrigibly generous. Once she took me to Partridge's in Bond Street and walked me through all the departments, asking me to choose anything I liked. Of course I blushingly refused, but she insisted on sending me a huge parcel of glass and china to help furnish a cottage which I had just taken in the country, and she would encourage me to bring my friends so that she might entertain them as well as myself when I came to her house. Taking a great fancy to one of them who was knowledgeable about the Turf (she had been a great huntress in her youth), she proceeded to present him with a horse.

Our friendship prospered for several years. She had a fine Lutyens house near Hastings, to which she would invite me for weekends, with glasshouses, rhododendrons and a water garden. Her Rolls, driven by an elderly and trusted chauffeur, would be waiting at the stage-door, and she would greet me, in jewels and evening dress, on the doorstep at one o'clock in the morning, with a hot supper waiting to be served as soon as I arrived.

She told me she had been married to the 'richest commoner in England' but I gathered she had not been greatly fond of him, and she hinted at a passionate love-affair with one of her grooms, whose subsequent death had shattered her. She also had several daughters to whom she referred with considerable disapproval, but I never met any of her family.

She was extremely good company, suddenly surprising one with frank and unexpected remarks delivered without a hint of malice. 'He powders his face. I fear he will have to go,' she murmured to me one day as the butler was busy at the other end of the table. On another occasion, when a young priest was one of the guests she announced to the assembled party, 'Father B. is a saint. He has started a Home for Unwanted Boys. Imagine anyone not wanting a boy.' And once I heard her remark, as one of my actress friends was out of hearing, 'Ah, I fear it is evident that C. aime les femmes.'

She took me several times to Glyndebourne, then in the great inaugural days of John Christie, Busch and Ebert, and during the interval we walked across the garden to a field close by, where a sumptuous supper was laid out, specially sent over from her house in a horse-box, with flowers, silver and a lace tablecloth, upright chairs, and a footman to wait on us.

About this time, however, her interest began to seem somewhat less concentrated where I was concerned, for she had been greatly attracted to a young Indian just down from Oxford, and I was somewhat dismayed when, during one of the opera performances at Glyndebourne, she slipped a flask of perfume into my hand, whispering that I should pass it to him to sprinkle on his hands. He had aspired to become a ballet dancer, but it soon appeared that he was not strong enough to lift his partners and was forced to abandon his ambitions in that direction. He was certainly strikingly good-looking, and changed his suits and jewellery several times a day, but I was not greatly sorry when his reign appeared to be over and I was restored to the best bedroom, from which I had been temporarily superseded, when I went to stay.

In 1936, when I went to New York to play Hamlet, my benefactress soon followed me in order to be present at my first night. She stayed at the Plaza Hotel, accompanied by a maid who sat with the chauffeur as she drove about the city, shopping and visiting museums and galleries and investigating religious groups. When the great night arrived, she appeared in the foyer, splendidly arrayed, some minutes before the rise of the curtain, and was immediately interviewed and photographed by reporters who were convinced she was my mother. On my return from America she insisted on giving a big dinner party in my honour, to which she invited my parents and a dozen of my best friends.

When war broke out in 1939, she was still going strong. Of course I never knew her real age, but she had joined the WRNS as an officer, and very fine and dignified she looked as she greeted me at the door in her uniform and tricorne hat worn with a martial air. I do not remember seeing her again after that day, for she died while I was abroad, and the short obituary that was afterwards forwarded to me gave little information about her early life. Her houses were both sold soon afterwards, the Sussex house dismantled and the gardens and grounds hacked up for a building development, which would have made her very sad. I still possess a number of charming presents that she gave me at various times. Several of my most elegant books are dedicated in her characteristic manner, and the sight of her strong handwriting always reminds me vividly of her energy and charm, her endless generosity, the way she accepted so many of my friends, never dreaming of interfering, influencing or intruding in any way. She was known in her heyday as 'the fascinating Mrs – and that is how I shall always think of her.

14

QUEEN MARY

The Royal Family, with the notable exceptions of Queen Elizabeth the Queen-Mother, and the late Queen Mary, have not been very enthusiastic playgoers during the last fifty years, though Queen Victoria loved the theatre in her youth, and as an elderly lady commanded quite a number of plays to be performed for her at Windsor, when the Waterloo Chamber was temporarily transformed, and the Court sat deferentially anxious, waiting to see whether her Majesty was amused or moved. The actor-managers, Irving, Hare and others, had simplified scenery specially made for these occasions and closed their London theatres for the night in order to comply with the Royal Command.

Edward VII was mostly fond of comedies, and basked in the lighter aspect of the Paris theatres, where he was often to be found both in the auditorium and behind the scenes (he is even said to have once appeared as the dying husband in the first act of Bernhardt's *Fedora*, where the character lies in a bed at the back of the stage), but Queen Alexandra was very deaf and preferred opera to the straight theatre. She herself had been an enthusiastic amateur pianist, and I once met an old lady in Washington who told me she used sometimes to be invited to stay at Sandringham in order to play duets with her while King Edward was out shooting.

But Shakespeare and the Classics have always, I fancy, been somewhat of a strain upon Royal endurance. (The Duke of Windsor once asked me about the plays of T. S. Eliot. 'Were they not in verse?' he wanted to know. I replied somewhat nervously that I believed Eliot himself referred to them as 'staggered verse'. 'Ah, yes,' he said, 'of course a lot of Shakespeare's in verse, too.') Queen Mary had been an ardent playgoer in her young days, and sometimes attended Henry Irving's Beefsteak supper parties after visits to his Lyceum productions with her mother, the Duchess of Teck. Later, when she became Queen, she was obliged to be seen at a few serious plays, as well as greatly enjoying light comedies and even thrillers. In her last years she went a great deal to the theatre, and her approval of a piece called *Pick-up Girl*, which she visited on more than one occasion, brought headlines in the press and a corresponding reaction at the box-office.

King George V, like his mother, was deaf, and was said to enjoy his playgoing chatting about racing with Sir Edward Elgar at the back of the box. Arriving for a charity matinée of *Hamlet* at the Haymarket Theatre one afternoon, Queen Mary asked the head of the Reception Committee what time the performance would be over. 'You see,' she said, 'the King always has to have his tea punctually, and he is so anxious not to miss seeing the girl with the straws in her hair.'

King George did not accompany the Queen when she went to the Old Vic one evening, and Lilian Baylis, standing beside her in the box as the sad little orchestra squeaked through the National Anthem, was heard to remark comfortingly, 'You see, madam, we always play your husband's little tune.'

Queen Mary had a wonderful presence, and the audience (as well as the players, if they dared) delighted to watch her, as she sat with her opera-glasses raised steadily in a white gloved hand, during the whole performance. I was lucky enough to be presented to her several times when she came to see plays that I was acting in, and I have a vivid picture of her in the retiring-room at the Globe Theatre, when several of us had been sent for after the first act of *The Importance of Being Earnest*, just before the war. The Queen, half a head shorter than Edith Evans, looked almost like her on a small scale, and when Edith curtseyed one felt she should really have curtseyed back.

When she came one evening to Chekhov's *The Three Sisters* at the Queen's Theatre, a year or two earlier, we all wondered what she would make of the Russian gloom. I was to be presented after the second act, and sent word asking if I might bring my four leading ladies with me. Of course the answer came back 'yes', but I went up to the retiring-room alone while the ladies changed. Queen Mary came out from the box and I gasped in admiration at her appearance. She wore a glittering dress of black paillettes, and a magnificent set of aquamarines with matching earrings, necklace, and bracelets. Perhaps a tiara, too, but I am not sure of this. I know I longed to touch her to see if she was real. She was exceedingly shy and I fancy she spoke with a faint German accent. At any rate her voice was gruff and rather brusque. The ladies arrived and we made desultory conversation, mostly about their stage costumes, for five minutes or so. The Queen then said she felt sure we must get back for the next act, and there was some confusion as we all tried to back out of the retiring-room together through a very small door. One of the ladies, Carol Goodner, an American, who was particularly nervous and excited, backed through the wrong door to the Royal lavatory and had to be extricated before she could beat a hasty retreat. Then, as I was leaving with a bow, the Queen remarked with an enchanting smile, 'Well, I suppose it all ends very badly.' Not a bad summing-up of Chekhov after only two acts.

During the war years when she stayed at Badminton, Queen Mary was fond of giving lifts in her car to soldiers she met on the road, which, naturally, endeared her to the whole neighbourhood, and she often asked actors who came to play at the camps to give performances for her and her entourage at Badminton House. She even came to some of the troop shows and sat amongst the men in a big armchair.

My favourite story of her may or may not be apocryphal. Walking one day in the garden at Buckingham Palace, King George enquired why his usual equerry was not in attendance. He was told that the man was ill and the King asked what was the matter. 'Oh, the universal complaint, sir,' was the evasive reply. Next day Queen Mary remarked to someone, 'I hear the King's equerry is ill. What is the matter with him?' 'A severe attack of haemorrhoids, I'm afraid, ma'am.' 'Oh!' said the Queen, 'why did the King tell me it was the clap?'

My last memory of her was in 1951, when she came to a matinée of *The Winter's Tale* at the Phoenix Theatre. Diana Wynyard, Flora Robson, Lewis Casson and I were presented during the first interval when just after Leontes accuses Hermione of adultery she swoons and appears to be dead.

The Queen seemed very interested in the play. She shook Lewis Casson warmly by the hand. 'Of course, I've often seen you before.' Then turning to Diana Wynyard, 'You wrote me a very nice letter when the King died. I hope you got my answer.' And finally to me. 'Well, it's extremely well done, your part, but extremely unpleasant, of course.'

15

NEW YORK

I have always loved cities – first London, where I was born and lived for seventy years, then Oxford, New York, and Venice, in that order. I had always longed to work in America, and it has never disappointed me, from the first time I went there, so long ago, in 1928, to act in a play which only ran a week.

Luckily, however, before I went back home (since I could not, at that time, afford to stay) I saw something of the Broadway theatre, flourishing and lively as it was in those days – Helen Hayes in *Coquette*, Judith Anderson in *Behold the Bridegroom*, and, standing at the back of the orchestra in the new Ziegfeld Theatre among a packed matinée audience, I watched with rapture the original production of *Show Boat*, with Norma Terris, Howard Marsh, Charles Winninger, Jules Bledsoe, Edna May Oliver, and, best of all, Helen Morgan as Julie singing 'Bill' on the top of a piano with a long chiffon handkerchief dangling from her wrist. Mabel Mercer was at Tony's in 52nd Street and there were speak-easies, the Cotton Club, evenings in Harlem, the dining room at the Hotel Algonquin packed with celebrities, and unexpected meetings with English players I knew who were acting in New York. No wonder I have always vividly remembered that first short visit with wonder and delight. Today, after living there very often over many years, I am still stimulated by the unpredictable, electric liveliness of the city, despite the extremes of heat and cold, cramped taxis and sweltering buses, the squalor of the subways, the steam-heating and air conditioning, the friendliness and politeness (as well as the occasional rudeness), the foreignness mixed with familiarity. I love the brilliant quality of the New York lights, from twinkling towers as they begin to glitter on Central Park South round six o'clock on a winter evening – and the strip of sky which one can always see in four directions even from the deep canyons of the avenues. The vista of Fifth Avenue from St Patrick's Cathedral to the Plaza Hotel is, to me, one of the finest sights in the world, with an elegance that our own Bond Street used once to have but has now lost forever, smothered as it is today by so many cheap new shops and unimaginative modern buildings.

American theatres dismayed me at first with their extreme width of auditorium and shallow stages – no bars or proper lounges (save for those cavernous overheated cellars, with queues lining up for the telephone in the intermissions) and the disagreeable men who tear up one's tickets as one passes through the doors in the narrow entrance halls. Yet the sense of expectation in an American audience – especially at matinées when the women predominate, screaming and waving greetings to one another across the aisles, and wildly applauding every entrance and exit, song or dance – is wonderfully infectious and finally rewarding, both for actors and spectators alike, and infinitely preferable to the scene in London, where trays of tea are shuffled in and out over people's heads, and the elderly ladies sit munching with dogged indifference, often slumbering and even snoring as the afternoon wears on.

I have, alas, no memories of seeing the great actors and actresses of America as I have of so many in England, though Guthrie McClintic used to entertain me with wonderful stories of Mrs Fiske and Emily Stevens, Nazimova and Laurette Taylor, all alas before my time.

PAULINE LORD, JOHN BARRYMORE, JANE COWL, LESLIE HOWARD

I happened to be present on the first night of a new play *Salvation* by Sidney Howard at the Empire Theatre in New York. I remember little of the play save a splendid performance by Osgood Perkins father of the film star Anthony

Perkins as a newspaperman, and the strange broken syllables and emotional power of Pauline Lord, who played the leading part.

I had seen her once before at the Strand Theatre in London (also, oddly enough, on the opening night) when she played O'Neill's *Anna Christie* and took the town by storm. But when Greta Garbo made her huge success in the film version of the play, Pauline Lord's wonderful acting was soon forgotten, though not by me. Years later, I was leaving the Plaza Hotel in New York by a side door one afternoon, when I recognised Miss Lord, sitting in an armchair in the passageway, looking extremely sad and lonely. I ventured to introduce myself, and her face lit up with pleasure when I reminded her of her triumph in London. But she told me she had lost heart for the theatre, and had just returned from playing Amanda (the mother) in a tour of Tennessee Williams's *The Glass Menagerie*, which I imagine she must have acted brilliantly, though eclipsed, I suppose, as far as New York was concerned at any rate, by comparison with the great Laurette Taylor who created the part on Broadway, an actress whom, alas, I never saw. Pauline Lord's pathos was extraordinary, individual and evocative, and I often think of her strange beauty on the stage.

I greatly admired John Barrymore as Hamlet when I saw him in London in 1926, and once heard him speak at a Sunday Dinner Club, but I never met him, though he sent me a page-long telegram when I was honoured ten years later at a dinner in New York by the Players Club. His famous sister Ethel I met several times at George Cukor's house in Beverly Hills in her last years, but I never saw her act except on the screen.

Jane Cowl I met in London, and saw her when she played Noël Coward's *Easy Virtue* there in 1926. Miss Cowl was most effective in the Coward play, and adapted her acting style to great advantage in modern plays after successes in New York both as Juliet and Cleopatra. She was also very dramatic in private life. She fainted one night when she was in the audience watching John Barrymore in Galsworthy's *Justice*. A few weeks later someone told Barrymore 'Jane Cowl is in front again.' 'Is she?' Barrymore remarked airily. 'I do hope she'll give a good performance.'

While she was in England, Miss Cowl wrote a play under the pen name C. R. Avery entitled *Hervey House*. It was presented at His Majesty's Theatre in May 1935, with an all-star cast headed by Fay Compton and Gertrude Lawrence. (I was nearly in the play myself in the role eventually played by Nicholas Hannen.) Margaret Rutherford made one of her first successes in a supporting part, as did Alan Webb, but *Hervey House* did not achieve a long run although it was brilliantly directed by Tyrone Guthrie. During the weeks they were awaiting rehearsals, Fay Compton and Gertrude Lawrence made a tour of Devonshire riding bicycles, while a Rolls-Royce followed them distantly in case they became tired.

The year 1936 when I played Hamlet at the Empire Theatre in New York for Guthrie McClintic (with Lillian Gish, Judith Anderson, and Arthur Byron) was, of course, one of the most exciting of my life, though I was placed in a somewhat embarrassing position when Leslie Howard appeared during the same season in his own production and with a number of English players in his cast. (Malcolm Keen and Harry Andrews who played the King and Horatio respectively were the only English actors in mine.)

Howard had announced that he had decided not to put on the play before I had agreed to come over in the spring of that year, but later changed his mind, and I was upset at having to compete with a fellow countryman whom I did not know but greatly admired, and who was also an internationally popular film star. The reviews for my performance were encouraging but not wholly enthusiastic, and I was expecting a run of not more than a few weeks. When Howard opened, however, a few weeks later, and was poorly received, our performances began to sell out almost immediately. The press tried to persuade us to meet and give interviews about one another, but we stuck to our own guns and behaved with as much dignity as possible. Still, the Battle of the Hamlets was quite a popular topic in the city for several months. Beatrice Lillie played in a sketch about us in a revue, and even the taxi drivers used to ask which of the Hamlets I was when I directed them to the stage door of the Empire. The abdication of the Duke of Windsor, which happened at the same time, helped to fascinate the New York public with

England and Royalty, everyone arguing and taking sides.

I have been lucky enough, through my work in the theatre, to meet four American Presidents. Lillian Gish took me to see President and Mrs Roosevelt at the White House, and I met Truman, Johnson, and Kennedy on different occasions when they came to see plays that I was appearing in. During the *Hamlet* run I did not keep a diary, and find it hard to remember the many fascinating and illustrious visitors who were kind enough to come round to see me.

But two amusing incidents have always remained with me. One night, when I was very tired at the end of two performances, Maria Ouspenskaya, an elderly Russian actress, was announced. I had greatly admired her in films, particularly *Dodsworth* and *The Rains Came*, and she had recently been acting in the theatre in New York in a Greek tragedy, though I had not been fortunate enough to see it. She came into the dressing-room, a formidable and striking personality with a long cigarette holder in her hand, looking very distinguished and escorted by an elegant young man who leaned gracefully against the wall behind her. 'Oh, Madame Ouspenskaya,' I burst out, gathering my dressing gown about me and wondering if I ought to kiss her hand, 'I am so sorry to think you were in front tonight. I was dreadfully tired and I know I played so badly!' On which Madame nodded her head twice in profound approval, turned around, and left the room without a word.

On another evening, Judith Anderson brought in a friend of hers to see me, a Swedish Countess beautifully bejewelled and dressed. She seemed greatly moved by the performance and, as she was leaving, murmured, 'I would like to give you something in remembrance of this great experience,' and, putting out her hand, began to take off a most beautiful square cut emerald ring that she was wearing. I nervously began to put out my own hand, but, just as I did so, she hastily drew her ring back on to her finger and made a graceful exit. I thought I must have imagined the whole episode, but Judith Anderson assured me afterwards that it was perfectly true.

The generosity of the leading players in America has always charmed me. When I opened in *Hamlet* I received telegrams of good wishes from a number of stars whom I had never even met, and on the last night, Helen Hayes, who was playing *Victoria Regina* so brilliantly at the Broadhurst Theatre just opposite, sent over a tray, with a bottle of champagne and glasses, saying how sorry she was that I was leaving this neighbourhood. I have the happiest memories of the Players Club, the courtesy of its late presidents, Walter Hampden, Howard Lindsay, and Dennis King, and the dinners given there for me, and on other occasions for Alfred Lunt and Lynn Fontanne, and for Howard Lindsay just before his death. I was given a degree a few years ago at Brandeis University in Massachusetts and made a freeman of the City of Philadelphia, and I need hardly say that I have always found America, and Hollywood too – on the few occasions I have worked there – to be immensely kind and encouraging. I shall always look on that country as my second home, where I have made so many delightful friends among my fellow players and the audiences for whom I have played.

16

PROMENADE

In July 1919 I was still a schoolboy of fifteen, a dayboy at Westminster, living at home with my parents, but proud possessor of my first latchkey. Already irredeemably stage-struck, I was bent on designing scenery and costumes for the stage, torn between admiration for the drawings of my cousin, Gordon Craig, and the romantic and more conventional staging of *Chu Chin Chow*, the oriental musical panto-mime which reflected the illustrations of Edmund Dulac and Kay Nielsen that I had so loved as a boy, and which I had even tried to copy in my own amateurish way. I had bought several volumes of Aubrey Beardsley drawings too (which I found wildly exciting as well as somewhat decadent and improper) and had become an eager admirer of Compton MacKenzie's *Sinister Street*, with its nostalgic picture of pre-war Oxford and later excursions into Bohemian London, especially as I had caught one of the masters at my prep-school reading the novel surreptitiously, hidden discreetly beneath a brown paper cover. In short, I was longing to experience every kind of adolescent discovery, especially with regard to the theatre, though I had yet no desire or thought of becoming an actor myself.

I was a great walker in those days, finding my way all over London – Lincoln's Inn, Chelsea, Chiswick, Kew Gardens and Hampton Court among many favourite excursions – but my Mecca was the West End and the triangle of streets radiating from Piccadilly Circus, where so many theatres stood. Were those old women in straw hats and shawls still sitting round the base of Eros selling flowers, in those last

years of the Great War? I well remember seeing them there,
but perhaps it was at an earlier period in my boyhood.

How I used to love jumping on to the top of a number 14
bus near our house in South Kensington and jumping off
again at the top of Piccadilly. On the way we passed Devonshire House, then an imposing edifice behind its elaborate
gates, and Solomon's the grand fruit shop next to the Berkeley
Hotel, its windows crammed with peaches, pineapples and
muscat grapes. Once arrived at the Circus I would begin my
favourite round. I would glance up the curve of Regent Street
for a glimpse of the portico of the Café Royal, where I had
once been taken by my brother when he was on leave during
the War. Here I had gaped at Augustus John, in a black
sombrero and gold earrings, sitting with his cronies among
the marble-topped tables and gilded caryatids, and there was
a kiosk with all the foreign newspapers on the ramp which
led from the street up to the brasserie, where, hanging on the
walls, the letter 'N' (for Nicole) was surrounded by gilt laurel
leaves. 'What does "N" stand for?' I asked my brother.
'Nature,' he replied, and led me to the Men's room.

I would walk up Shaftesbury Avenue, skirting on my left
the narrow streets of Soho (where I had occasionally ventured,
to show off my growing independence by ordering a delicious
lunch for seven and sixpence in an atmosphere mysteriously
foreign) but ignoring, to the right-hand side, the temptations
of Gerrard Street and Lisle Street, where the tarts lingered
provocatively all day long, as well as at night, attempting to
inveigle every man who passed. At Cambridge Circus I
would turn to the right down Charing Cross Road, with its
seedy but fascinating secondhand bookshops, and stroll down
St Martin's Lane as far as Trafalgar Square. Back again up
the Haymarket, and then through Panton Street to Leicester
Square. These walks round theatreland (still rather prim and
dignified in those days) allowed me to examine minutely all
the photographs and bills outside the playhouses, while I tried
to decide which seemed the most likely to encourage me to
invest my pocket-money and to savour the never-ending
delight of standing in a queue for several hours waiting for
the pit and gallery doors to open.

There were four theatres in those days in Leicester Square.
Daly's (replaced today by the Warner Brothers' Cinema)

stood close by the Hippodrome. A few doors off was the
Empire, then a famous Music Hall, whose notorious promenade was closed to ladies during the 1914 war, expelling the
throng of pretty ladies, who plied their trade there into outer
darkness and the rainy streets.

In the middle of the square stood the statue of Shakespeare,
improbably surveying his somewhat raffish surroundings.
The statue still remains today, flanked by a few trees, some
ill-kept grass, and two prominent public lavatories. But where
the Odeon Cinema now rears its majestic front, on one side of
the Square, was the old Alhambra Theatre, a pseudo-Moorish
edifice crowned by twin domes with gilded crescent moons
decorating their tops.

The theatre had mostly housed revues during the First War,
its most successful productions being *The Bing Boys are Here*
and *The Bing Boys on Broadway*, both of which starred a
famous team of comedians, George Robey, Alfred Lester and
Violet Loraine. The great song hit, *If You Were the Only Girl
in the World*, sung by Robey and Miss Loraine in the first
revue, was soon to be sung and whistled all over the world.
Inside, the building was crammed with arches, mosaics, and
tiled walls, and there was a big circular promenade at the back
of the stalls, similar to the one at the Empire, from which
women had been excluded after considerable publicity and
fuss. Here the admission price was five shillings. You could
lean on the cushioned edge which ran all round the back of
the seats and there were banquettes against the wall behind
you and big glass doors through which people slipped into
the great bar.

I had been once to *The Bing Boys on Broadway* at a matinée,
sitting grandly with my family in a box near the stage, but
the Promenade was quite a new point of vantage, and it was
to the Promenade that my father decided to take me, on that
memorable summer evening in 1919, to see the Diaghilev
Russian Ballet Company for the first time.

I always regretted bitterly that I was too young to have
seen the legendary genius, Nijinsky, who had left Diaghilev
just before the War, but I had seen Anna Pavlova on one
or two occasions, and had been ravished by her brilliant
personality, though unimpressed by her material, which
seemed, even to my young eyes, somewhat conventional and

unimaginative, and by her supporting company, which I felt
to be somewhat second-rate. What I was to see tonight was
something very different. The programme consisted of three
halfhour ballets – Carnaval, La Boutique Fantasque and Prince
Igor, wonderfully contrasted in style and content, each one
more thrilling than the other. Karsavina had returned to the
Company, but was now only playing second parts. Leonide
Massine was the new principal male dancer and choreo-
grapher, and Tchernicheva and Lopokova, two of the leading
ballerinas, were to vie for my affections for many years to
come.

I had no knowledge of the technique of ballet dancing, and
to this day I am no judge of the fine points which are so dear
to critics and true balletomanes alike. But the entrancing
mixture of music, mime and spectacle enraptured me immediately, though at first I was somewhat puzzled by the décor –
by Bakst for Carnaval, Derain for the Boutique, Roerich for
Igor. The last was more immediately appealing – a line of low
tents under a lowering smoky sky. But Carnaval was set in
high flats of bluish-green wallpaper with a pattern of huge
flowers, almost like cabbages, sprawling over it, and towards
the back of the set two small blue sofas, in the Biedemeyer
style, stood side by side on an otherwise empty stage. For
Boutique the scenery was extremely avant-garde. A strange
drop curtain, with exaggerated figures drawn on it, rose to
reveal the interior of the toyshop, with enormously high
windows at the back through which one could see a painted
steamer. Shelves and plates, chairs and curtained windows
were drawn on the side-wings. It was all quite unrealistic and
at first I found it difficult to accept. But it did not take me
long to change my mind, for the combination of elements
was immediately entrancing. The ballets still used a lot of
pantomime (especially of course in story ballets like Cléopâtre,
Thamar, Schéhérazade, Petrushka and The Good-Humoured
Ladies, all of which I was to see and love on later visits), but,
even on this first experience, I was able to appreciate the
acting as well as the dancing, which seemed to merge together
with incredibly skilful ease and grace. Pierrot, in Carnaval,
trying to catch a butterfly in his cap, and the parents of the
children in Boutique, in which Cecchetti, the great choreo-
grapher for Diaghilev and his elderly wife, gave inimitable

performances as non-dancing characters. The detail was as fascinating as the verve and brilliance of the ensemble. The elegance of *Carnaval*, the high spirits of *Boutique*, with Lopokova as the chief Doll, in a white flounced dress, with a white and pink wreath on her head, rioting through the cancan to a sensational finish ending in the splits, and Massine – chalk-white face, long sideburns and a black velvet suit – a superbly accomplished partner, flinging himself about in his white socks and flying coat-tails. Finally the savage dances in *Prince Igor*, with the women spread out across the stage, waving their arms seductively, as the men, with their fierce moustaches and bows and arrows, leapt wildly up and down, now advancing on the girls, now jumping over them towards the front of the stage till one felt they would hurl themselves across the footlights into the auditorium, as the music crashed out with increasing shrillness and the curtain fell to tumultu-ous applause.

I left the theatre in a dream. Soon I was to become an aficionado for all the Diaghilev seasons that were to follow during the next three years, but nothing could ever quite equal the first sight of their originality and glamour. Standing in the Promenade beside my father and walking about with him in the intervals among the cigar smoke and clinking glasses all round me, I felt I had really grown up at last.

I seldom go to ballet any more. My memories of that first impact are too vivid and nostalgic, but they gave me an experience that has stayed with me unforgettably ever since.

17

CURTAIN CALLS

But what if there is no curtain, as is so often the case nowadays? The re-entrance of the cast for instance, as well as their subsequent difficulty in retiring at the end of the calls without turning their backs upon the audience, is quite a complicated manoeuvre on the wide expanses of the National Theatre's Olivier stage. And it is even more difficult for the stage management to judge the length of time to be allowed, according to the response of the spectators – whereas it is possible to gauge things more exactly with a curtain to rise and fall, and the actors can remain or redistribute themselves tidily on stage between times.

In America much attention is paid to the convention. Some years ago, when I was asked to direct a musical there (and was eventually sacked with some justification before it opened in New York) I quarrelled furiously with the impresario, who wasted valuable rehearsal time in devising elaborate curtain calls, though I ventured to protest that the old-fashioned 'walk down', so familiar to us in England in revues and pantomimes, would surely be a perfectly simple solution to the problem.

In the West End of London, during the early years of my career, the pit and gallery were always the accepted arbiters of applause, as well as making their voices heard if they considered the play unworthy of their approval. On first nights they would make their presence felt by greeting the celebrities among the audience as they made their way into the stalls. At the rise of the curtain there would be more clapping as a handsome setting was revealed, especially in spectacular costume plays and melodramas, while the entrance of the star would evoke a big round of applause, which the star would often acknowledge with a slight but gracious bow before he or she began to speak.

Right up to the early Thirties curtain calls were expected after every act, though the custom was gradually abandoned and began to be reserved for the end of the play. I remember being somewhat disconcerted when, in Sybil Thorndike's production of *Henry VIII* at the old Empire Theatre in the Thirties, Buckingham, Wolsey and Katharine each took individual calls immediately following their death scenes. And once, at a performance of *Tosca* in Verona, I was amazed to see the prima donna, after a passionate aria which ended in a fall to the ground, rise from the floor to bow in acknowledgment of the rapturous applause, and then resume a languid pose upon her sofa, from which she proceeded to repeat the aria, using exactly the same gestures and movements as before, and ending as before with a similar fall which left her prone upon the stage!

Three supreme exponents of the art of taking curtain calls were none of them straight actresses. Best of all, perhaps, was the great dancer, Anna Pavlova. After endless bows and the gracious acceptance of a mass of flowers, she would suddenly leap into the wings with a graceful bound, returning a few moments later from some other entrance at a different part of the stage. The applause would grow more and more frantic as she floated on and off, running, tiptoeing, or leaping, surprising the enraptured audience with every reappearance. Something of the same hysteria would greet the similar means used by Marlene Dietrich at the end of her solo performance, many years later, to encourage the applause. She too would leave the stage for several minutes, while the audience became gradually more insistent, and reappear unexpectedly from different entrances. She would allow a full twenty minutes for her calls, and managed the whole ceremony with a perfection of timing and execution. Maria Callas, on the other hand, would accept her ovations with an extraordinary command of personality; combining queenly dignity with an effect of grateful, and even humble, appreciation.

In my early days in the theatre, the curtain calls at the end of a play would sometimes degenerate into something of a shambles, as the director of the play – and the author too in a contemporary piece – were led on to the stage by the leading lady. Ill at ease in the glare of the footlights, and looking oddly inappropriate among the actors in their make-up and costumes, they were apt to be unrecognised by the audience. Their speeches too were often inept, and sometimes inaudible, and the leading players would follow them by obliging with a few tactful words. On a famous occasion, the opening night of Noël Coward's *Sirocco* – one of his few sensational failures – Frances Doble stepped forward and began, 'This is the happiest moment of my life' – to be speedily interrupted by yells of derision from the gallery.

But many of the star performers of that period were experts in delivering the curtain speeches so often demanded of them. Fred Terry, Martin Harvey and Matheson Lang charmed their audiences with appropriate compliments, and Donald Wolfit, who had studied their methods when he had been apprenticed to two of them, would stand, shaking the curtain to encourage the applause, before emerging in front of it to speak, dishevelled but triumphant and gasping with exhaustion. Marie Tempest would always grace her final curtain with an elegant curtsey, whereas Edith Evans seemed rather to disdain the whole convention and would acknowledge the audience with an air of somewhat tolerant resignation.

My own dislike of over-elaborate curtain calls springs perhaps from a production of *The School for Scandal*, at the end of which Tyrone Guthrie had spent much time in posing the actors in amusing groups. I remember that as Joseph Surface I had to wait until the cast was all assembled and then pop my head up over a screen – and *The Times* critic remarked, not unfairly, that after a rather untidy performance of the play itself, the company had evidently decided to join the Russian Ballet.

We know, of course, that in the eighteenth century the audience loved to applaud any points or innovations of business created by the great actors – Garrick, Macready and Edmund Kean – and they took calls after every scene.

It is curious that in America the custom of greeting favourites with applause is still continued, whereas in England it has markedly diminished. The hysteria of audiences seems to be reserved in this country for pop concerts, where the interruptions continue unceasingly before, during, and after the performance. Now that films and television have dispensed with audible reactions, applause may perhaps become less and less to be expected. And the lack of a curtain may necessitate a return to the directions of Shakespeare, for bodies must be ceremoniously borne off at the end of the classical tragedies. Otherwise the director must have recourse to a blacked-out stage, while the poor corpses must scurry into the wings in ignominious half-obscurity, before returning, safe and sound, to receive the plaudits of the audience.

But there is little doubt that most of us players can hardly fail to enjoy the age-long custom of curtain calls, and would feel cheated if they were obliged to forego them altogether. Audiences, too, perhaps. As Fred Terry used to say proudly in one of his curtain speeches:

'If there is anything an actor values more than your applause, it is your silent attention to detail that enables us to give you of our best.'

Plays and Players, 1985

18

PAUSE AND EFFECT

Today, when we are so overwhelmed by sound of every kind – aeroplanes, traffic, television, radio, transistors and loud-speakers all day long – the effect of silence, both on stage and screen, seems sadly to have become infinitely more significant than ever before. Many people find it menacing, lonely and depressing, but its power is undeniable. Strikingly used, it can be tragic, terrifying, nostalgic or evocative.

It can be comic, too. The great comedians – Chaplin, in whose performances silence is everything, George Robey, who paused as he surveyed the audience and had them roaring with laughter before he uttered a word – these geniuses and their successors can use the pause and illuminate a silence with an individual magic beyond words, while the new playwrights have learned to entrust their interpreters with equally pragmatic opportunities.

Modern playwrights make a tremendous effect with pauses, as I realised very quickly in the two plays *Home*, by David Storey, and *No Man's Land*, by Harold Pinter, in which I was lucky enough to appear. Pinter even prints his pauses explicitly in his texts, and the 'Pinter Pause' is now a kind of copyright in the theatre world as it was once the traditional property of the actor Macready in the nineteenth century.

'Pause' was the favourite interruption of the Russian director Theodore Komisarjevsky, when I first rehearsed for him in some early London productions of Chekhov in the Twenties. He was determined to orchestrate his productions as significantly in the silences as in the dialogue.

Bernard Shaw, on the other hand, though equally musical,

demanded continual attack and speed, though his ear was impeccably accurate and his text demanded extremely accurate execution. But in the acting of his wordy plays there is no time to waste, nor can one find an excuse for slow delivery and lengthy pauses in acting Congreve, Sheridan, Wilde, Maugham or even Noël Coward.

With Shakespeare it is another matter. The old actors seem to have made immense pauses to gain their best effects – Macready, Kean and especially Irving, whose diction and vocal weakness were evidently a continual hazard in his reading of the verse. Shaw was always attacking him for putting his Shakespearean performances in between the actual lines, and even Ellen Terry confessed to being obliged to change her timing to disadvantage when she played Portia and Beatrice in his productions.

Both Irving and Tree cut the Shakespearean texts ruthlessly in order to interpolate elaborate stage effects, and it was not till Granville-Barker's 1912-14 Savoy productions that audiences were allowed to hear full texts spoken at great speed, though, because of this innovation, the actors found it difficult to sustain the pace demanded of them, and the critics and public, used to the old-fashioned deliberate declamatory style, found the experiment new-fangled and complained of inaudibility.

Actors set great store by the art of timing. By this they mean the way they judge how to gain the most telling result from the speaking of a text at different speeds, in emphasising a particular word or phrase, and learning how to gauge their delivery with flexibility and skill, according to the reactions of their fellow players and the audience at every different performance.

The live rapport between a player and his public is a continual challenge and refreshment, and he is intensely receptive to the varying temper of the public as well as to the difference in the sizes of the theatres he may appear in, which may demand broader or more intimate methods.

In filming and television, of course, the art of timing is largely a matter for the director. The actors still rely on one another in their interplay, but the effects they achieve can easily be changed, without their knowledge, in subsequent cutting and editing. The timing of laugh-lines, in particular, is different and more uncertain without the reactions of a live audience, which is why, presumably, studio laughter and applause is so often dubbed in afterwards to create a more lively atmosphere in television comedies.

19

W. GRAHAM ROBERTSON

In the Tate Gallery there hangs a portrait of the young Graham
Robertson, one of Sargent's most striking successes – an
aesthetic-looking young man in a very long black overcoat
carrying a jade–handled ebony walking stick with a grey
poodle stretched out at his feet. (Robertson told me that
Sargent insisted on his taking off his clothes under the overcoat in order to look more slender in the portrait.)

It was in the early 1930s that I met him first, by then a
rather portly figure (though still addicted to wearing a Spanish
sombrero and a caped cloak), very benevolent and distinguished and living in a high narrow house on Campden
Hill.

I knew he had been one of Ellen Terry's greatest admirers,
and his reminiscences of the Lyceum (in his charming book
Time Was) during the great Irving days recall her with vivid
accuracy and grace. In the early years of this century she had
become one of his greatest friends, and had appeared at His
Majesty's as Aunt Imogen in his children's play, *Pinkie and
the Fairies* which was produced there by Sir Herbert Beerbohm
Tree one Christmas with considerable success. After her death
in 1927, Graham began to take a great interest in the young
players who were then beginning to be successful in London,
and he numbered Jean Forbes-Robertson, Eric Portman,
Ernest Milton and Marie Ney among those whom he
watched in the theatre and encouraged and entertained at his
home. He also wrote to me (I was then acting at the Old Vic)
and I went to tea with him in Kensington several times. I
was fascinated by his nostalgic anecdotes and was lost in

admiration of a water-colour by William Blake which hung over his mantelpiece, 'The River of Life', which depicted a young woman swimming with two children, and bearded elders in two temples on the bank looking on.

When Robertson left London for good he gave his splendid Blake collection to the Tate Gallery. He was a very rich man, but always seemed to me unostentatious and warm-hearted, though Gordon Craig writes bitterly in one of his books about Robertson's refusal to back one of Craig's few London productions at the beginning of the century. I imagine that, like most of Ellen Terry's friends and advisers, he had little confidence in giving money to her son, who was generally supposed to be suspect, unpractical, and extravagant, and had already squandered much of his mother's hard-earned savings in the unhappy season at the Imperial Theatre in 1901, when he produced Ibsen's *The Vikings* and *Much Ado* for her. Actually these failures were to be remembered long afterwards as important innovations as regards scenery and lighting and undoubtedly brought new originality, selectivity and a use of space to counteract the Edwardian fashion of elaborate display and attempted pictorial realism in the theatre.

Graham Robertson retired to live at Witley in a small house, with a charming garden and studio attached. Here he had always painted, and enjoyed producing several pageants featuring local talent. Ellen Terry would often stay with him there in her old age, when she had few men friends left. He was one of the oldest and most dependable who could still be relied on to give her rest and sympathy.

In 1942 I was suddenly invited to come down to Witley one Sunday with Alan Dent (then secretary to James Agate and theatre critic of the *News Chronicle*) and we set off together, standing in a crowded train, to be met by Robertson with a taxi at the station. We had been told beforehand that the War was a subject not to be mentioned, and he behaved as if the great crisis of the world had completely passed him by. He talked happily of his devotion to Alfred Lunt and Lynn Fontanne, who had recently become his friends when they had come over to act in London, and Ellen Terry's photograph stood in a place of honour on a little table with the inscription 'How happy I am to be at Sandhills!'

An elderly manservant opened the front door and later served a delicious lunch. But first we were taken into the kitchen to meet the cook, Mrs Cave, an august figure in black bombazine with a gold chain round her neck, and, I suspected, a handsome red wig. 'She nursed Carlyle when he was dying,' Graham whispered, and then, as we were ushered to a bedroom where a jug of hot water stood on a washstand with a towel folded over it (there was no hot water laid on in the house) he called out from below, 'The Blakes get less good as you go upstairs.' He walked us round his domain when lunch was over, and we had a most enchanting day. When I wrote afterwards to thank him, he wrote back: 'Perhaps you realised that you left London in 1942 and arrived some time in the 1890s.'

My mother, usually so appreciative of everyone, surprised me considerably, when I spoke to her with such enthusiasm of my new friendship, by saying 'Oh, yes, I remember him as being a very mother-ridden young man whom I sometimes used to meet sitting about in actresses' dressing-rooms.' But how well he was to write about these actresses afterwards!

Robertson was certainly no great painter, to judge by the pictures of his that I have seen, and he was, I suppose, something of a dilettante. But his taste was as evident as was the simple elegance which emanated from his distinguished personality, and I was very proud that he should take an interest in my own budding career. His writing has enormous charm and I am delighted that it should now engage the attention of a new generation, evoking, I hope, the same enthusiasm and enjoyment which I felt on reading it when it was published first.

October 1980

20

THE GLASS OF FASHION

Buried today in the drawers and cupboards of theatrical costumiers lie the paraphernalia of accessories, once so much a part of everyday use, in private life as well as on the stage, at the turn of the century and in the years before the First World War.

The muffs and fans (alas, Lady Windermere), the elbow-length gloves and cardcases, the button boots, braces, and spats, monocles, pince-nez and lorgnettes, the powder-puffs and cigarette-holders, inkwells, blotting pads and sealing wax, sugar-tongs, sock-suspenders, collar studs, all these are forgotten now. Whatever became of the smart shops which specialised in these objects, once so greatly in demand? With what delight, as a young playgoer, did I watch the elegant deportment of the older actors and actresses, as they sat on chairs and sofas, straightbacked with pointed feet, while the younger members of the cast lounged about, challenging their prim behaviour, the girls crossing their legs in their short skirts, while the young men, in their blue blazers and flapping white flannel trousers, charged through the inevitable french windows, brandishing their tennis rackets, balancing jauntily on the furniture, tapping their cigarette-cases to point their lines and blowing smoke through their noses as they offered a 'fag' to their partners.

No longer can one see a witty actress dabbing her nose with a tiny handkerchief trimmed with lace, so useful to tease and provoke their partners in scenes of flirtation, quarrelling, or social chit-chat, while the men would also produce large white handkerchiefs from sleeve or starched cuff wherewith to mop their brows or proffer to a damsel in distress. Kleenex, however useful and hygienic, is hardly a very attractive substitute.

At what date, I wonder, did ladies, and especially actresses, begin to admit that they suffered from poor eyesight? In 1934, when I was beginning to venture into the task of directing plays, the beautiful Isobel Jeans, whom I had so often admired as a young playgoer, agreed to appear in a play of Emlyn Williams which I was to stage. After the first rehearsal she drew from her bag a pair of large green horn-rimmed spectacles. When she was not peering through them to correct her lines, she would take them off from time to time and gesticulate with them to great effect.

Women on the stage never wore glasses unless they were playing frumps, and even in real life they would carry a lorgnette for use in the street or shopping, and opera glasses when they went to the theatre. Only very old ladies were occasionally to be seen wearing gold-rimmed spectacles (elderly men often wore monocles) and schoolgirls were often made to wear them by their parents, though they appeared to have discarded them for ever before they 'came out'. (The strange fad of 'granny-glasses' affected by young women only a few years ago did not, I am glad to say, appear to catch on.) Fashions have changed too in the discussion and portrayal of many other afflictions, and our permissive age has completely removed any hesitation to write about them, in plays as well as books, and we can refer to them unashamedly even in mixed company.

Blindness was always a sure engager of sympathy, especially in melodrama, though cripples could be pitied or equally arouse terror, from Richard the Third to The Hunchback of Notre Dame. False teeth were never mentioned of course, in polite society, and Somerset Maugham, in his comedy *The Circle* produced at the end of the First War, created a sensation (only equalled by Shaw's 'Not bloody likely' in *Pygmalion* as far back as 1915) when he made one of the characters rush out of the room with 'My damned teeth are coming out!' The music-hall comedians had of course found them a good excuse for laughter many years before (as well as mothers-in-law and kippers). In 1954, the authoress of *The Chalk Garden*, Enid Bagnold, demanded that her leading lady should announce her first entrance from off-stage, calling to her factotum, 'Are my teeth on the table? My bottom teeth . . .' and the management were doubtful of persuading any leading actress to accept the part. Fortunately Edith Evans in London, and Gladys Cooper in New York, managed to surmount embarrassment with remarkable expertise and handled the episode with remarkable grace and tact.

Deafness was always a good card to play. Feydeau employed it a great deal, and the Victorians sometimes used ear-trumpets, though I rarely remember seeing one in my youth. I imagine that Evelyn Waugh, who carried one and used it ostentatiously in his latter life, must have ordered it specially.

During the last few years there have been a succession of books, plays and newspaper articles, dealing with every kind of physical experience, deafness and dumbness, childbirth, operations to be read about and seen in the theatre and the television, to say nothing of morgues, funerals and masturbation.

21

MY FAVOURITE ROOM

For an actor, his dressing-room, in my case at any rate, is the centre of his existence during the hours he is committed to spend in it. So I can honestly call it my favourite room, though its features, in the many hundred different ones I have occupied over more than sixty years, must necessarily vary enormously from one theatre to another.

Of course in my early days I was always obliged to share a dressing-room with other actors, and was immensely gratified to have reached the privilege, in the late 1920s, of being given a room to myself, with my name proudly displayed upon the door.

My favourite room is in my favourite London theatre, the Haymarket. Although ideally it is preferable to dress as close to the stage as possible, this particular room is situated at the very top of the theatre, with a long flight of stairs leading up to it. It is almost like a small flat, with an anteroom and bathroom leading out of the main room, which has windows looking on to Suffolk Street far below. There are plenty of shelves and cupboards, chairs, a sofa and writing desk – even, until recent times, a coal fire in winter – and it is therefore possible to install oneself there comfortably, even occasionally in the daytime when there is no performance.

Here I dressed for a number of years in various productions, and in 1944, when the buzzbombs were such a disagreeable interruption, I would firewatch several nights a week, sleeping in my dressing-room at intervals. Garlands Hotel, only a few yards away, was hit and finally completely destroyed in two successive air raids, and I dreaded lest the theatre – so happily constructed, but mostly in wood and plaster – should also become a victim. I always wondered, too, if I should meet the famous Haymarket Ghost, during the watches of the night (said to be a famous old actor), but I never succeeded in seeing him, though Margaret Rutherford once claimed that she did.

The privacy of a star dressing-room gives its occupant a very pleasant promise of relaxation, although the routine of making-up, now a much simpler process than was once thought necessary, demands the necessary tedium of looking at one's face in the glass for half-an-hour or so. But this is perhaps a less depressing prospect than the similar routine while shaving every morning.

The other London theatres in Shaftesbury Avenue and Charing Cross Road, mostly built at the turn of the century, are fortunately pretty well equipped with spacious and convenient dressing-rooms, whereas at Stratford-on-Avon, and more recently, at the mammoth new houses at the National and the Barbican, they are amazingly ill-designed, cramped and uncomfortable. One cannot imagine that the plans for them would have been passed by experienced eyes.

The Broadway theatres in New York are also, for the most part, equally gloomy and claustrophobic, while in Philadelphia I once played in a theatre where the dressing-rooms had been forgotten altogether, and the actors had to content themselves with rooms on the other side of the street and toil along a passage underground in order to reach the stage.

But I have always looked forward to arriving at the stage-door, well before curtain time, to find my dresser laying out my dressing-table and costumes in correct order, to put on a dressing-gown, open my mail, and sit before the mirror knowing exactly how long I need to prepare for my performance. Even in times of great stress, nervousness, despondency, failure or success, my dressing-room is a refuge from outside interference and I even resent it when the telephone rings.

In the old days I always anticipated the callboy's knock with a mixture of pleasure and dismay, although that long-established character has now ceased to exist, and the insistent barking of the tannoy system which has replaced it is for me a most unattractive and impersonal substitute in this progressive world.

With regard to dressing-room visitors I have rather mixed feelings, knowing that they can often mislead one into supposing that a performance has been very successful when it has been nothing of the kind. They feel they must attempt to be tactfully complimentary at all costs, and one is apt to be suspicious if they are unduly enthusiastic. Interviewers with tape-recorders, long-forgotten acquaintances, insincere flatterers, importunate authors with their manuscripts, and the occasionally impertinent unknown fan – these are occupational hazards, and one needs a devotedly tactful dresser to deal with them and ration their intrusions to as short a time as possible. And yet one is vain enough to be somewhat disappointed if no one comes to the dressing-room at the end of the performance, so long as they have the sense not to outstay their welcome.

The traditional ghosts at the Haymarket and Drury Lane are curious reminders of the great players who appeared in those theatres so long ago. At Her Majesty's and Wyndhams I dressed in rooms once occupied by Herbert Tree and Gerald du Maurier, and I felt proud to use those rooms so many years afterwards. And, in the last play in which I appeared in London, I found myself working for the first time in the Duke of York's Theatre, where I had seen my very first play *Peter Pan* when I was still a boy. So that those rooms backstage will always have a particular nostalgia for me, especially in the West End of London, where I so longed to appear and finally achieved that ambition over so many years. Will my own ghost linger in some of those dressing-rooms one day, I wonder?

22

ON ACTING SHAKESPEARE

A discussion with George Rylands

GEORGE RYLANDS: What were your first important Shakespeare roles, who directed them, and where were they played?

SIR JOHN GIELGUD: I played Romeo when I was nineteen at the Regent Theatre, long pulled down, under Barry Jackson's management, with Gwen Ffrangcon-Davies as Juliet. H. K. Ayliff, who was Jackson's great stand-by as a director, directed it. He was very hard with us, and I remember we played the dress rehearsal with the safety curtain down because Jackson had invited an audience and Ayliff thought the play was not ready for the audience. It wasn't very helpful for the poor actors to play to a safety curtain, and it was a pretty good disaster; it only ran about six weeks. I found it frightfully exhausting. I was very fond of myself at the time and fancied I was going to look very romantic, and found I didn't when I was made-up. It was fun in a way, but I got very bad notices, and it was after that, when I went to Fagan's repertory company in Oxford that I began to learn to act a bit. It was really much too soon to play such an important part, and so it was a big set-back for me, which I think did my conceit a lot of good.

RYLANDS: But Romeo is a poet and this might have been the moment when your famous speaking voice first made its impact on the world?

GIELGUD: I don't know. Ivor Brown said I was like Bunthorne, I remember; and I played Romeo after that two or three times and never felt I had a success in it. And when

Laurence Olivier and I played Mercutio and Romeo alter-
nately in 1935 in a very successful production, I was enraged
by the fact that he, who I knew didn't speak verse as well as
I did, was so much better as Romeo, because, as I think
Richardson said to me at the time, he only had to stand against
the balcony to convey the whole passionate emotion of this
animal lover. I was very cold and very voice-conscious and
very self-conscious, so I never really had a success with the
part of Romeo. But we were a very good team and it was
one of the first big productions when I directed myself as well
as acted.

RYLANDS: Did you find that to direct yourself in Shakespeare
is dangerous?

GIELGUD: It is dangerous because I pay far too much attention to the lights and the other people. On the other hand
when it comes off, as it did I think in *Much Ado* many years
later, you have the feeling you are the controlling force all
over the stage. You also have the fun of playing every night
and checking what goes on around you. Every few nights I
make a few notes – a very few – and if you go on doing that
carefully for a month, you find the improvement all round is
enormous; whereas if suddenly the director comes from outside and says the whole show's gone to pot, you have a rather
lazy and sullen rehearsal and often you can't get the show
back into its proper state. On the other hand, of course, one
is inclined, through doing that, to pay too much attention to
the others and not to concentrate on one's own part, which
is a dangerous thing to do, particularly in a big Shakespeare
part.

RYLANDS: What other great productions have there been in
your whole career?

GIELGUD: The first time I worked with Peter Brook we did
Measure for Measure, in a season when I played Angelo,
Cassius, Benedick, and Lear at Stratford in 1950, and they
were all, if I may say so, more or less successful. Brook was
awfully clever at knowing when I was false. One wants to be
told when one is bad and false, but one doesn't want to be
put down so that one loses confidence. And he has a way of
doing that, as Barker had and as you had; which is very
important – otherwise it's very easy to feel that you can't do
it at all, and then you lose all confidence and can't do it.

RYLANDS: What about some disasters?

GIELGUD: There was the Japanese *Lear*, which was considered to be a great disaster; we toured it on the Continent
and played at the Palace Theatre in London to packed houses,
and the young people and the avant-garde saw there was
something to it. I was accused of terrible gimmickry and the
only thing that pleased me about it was that, when Brook
did his *Lear* with Paul Scofield years later, he said to me very
generously that it was our *Lear* which had given him the basic
idea for his production, which was acknowledged to be
enormously successful, and it was true. The great mistake I
made in the Japanese *Lear* was a purely technical one. Noguchi, who was a sculptor, designed the sets and sent them to
us and we thought they were thrilling and I still think they
were, but I did not know at the time that he had never
designed costumes. He arrived with no costumes, he designed
them very hastily, he left before he had seen the fittings, he
was not at the dress rehearsal or the first night. We all looked
so strange and peculiar and I remember saying to George
Devine who was directing the play: 'Don't you think we
could discard all the costumes and get some rubber sheets and
make them into drapes and all wear sort of nondescript cloaks?
I believe with this scenery that might work.' And I still believe
it might have done; but we hadn't the courage at the last
moment to make such a drastic alteration, so I went through
with it because I felt Noguchi was too individual and brilliant
a designer to throw overboard completely, or half throw
overboard which would be even more dishonest.

RYLANDS: Yes, you couldn't do that. Now, one more disaster if you can bear me to mention it, and that is the Zeffirelli
Othello.

GIELGUD: This was a bitter blow to me because I've wanted
all my life to play Othello, although I'm quite sure the public
would never think me a satisfactory Othello in every way
because I haven't got what Agate used to call the thew and
sinew. Zeffirelli made the fatal mistake of dressing me as a
Venetian, so that I looked, as many of the notices said, like
an Indian Civil Servant. I didn't stand out from the others.
Desdemona was over-dressed, I was under-dressed, there was
much too much scenery, there were I think very damaging
cuts, and certain other members of the cast were to my mind

fatal. And it was terribly badly lit, which was very strange for Zeffirelli. He had dark scenery, so that with my dark face and dark clothes people couldn't see me – and when one feels one is not well lit, one is immediately at a disadvantage. He also did some terribly dangerous things like putting me far too much upstage; he had a wonderful-looking scene with a huge table and imprisoned me behind it so I couldn't get any contact with the audience or with the other actors. I felt that I only succeeded in the last scene of the play, when the poetry could carry me along. He had never seen me act, he had only seen me do the Shakespeare recital, so I don't think he knew at all what my dangers are when I act in a play, and he wasn't able to give me – or even Peggy Ashcroft – the right sort of confidence. We both suffered bitterly although we were both devoted to him and he had boundless universal charm. He consulted me to some extent over the cuts, but he put the intervals in fatal places. He insisted on having an interval after the first act, which he put at the end of the Senate scene where the play has hardly begun, and then we had a twenty-five-minute interval before Cyprus, which was disastrous. And he had very elaborate sets in the last act which made pauses between every scene – of course in opera houses, which he is used to, scenery can be moved more quickly and there can be much longer intervals. In Italy they have no idea of time, everything begins half an hour late and the intervals don't seem to matter because they're always great social occasions.

RYLANDS: You did a *Lear* production in which Granville-Barker had a hand, didn't you?

GIELGUD: He refused to take the full responsibility for it. This was just at the time of the fall of France in 1941. Tyrone Guthrie and Lewis Casson agreed to try to get Barker to come and work on the *Lear*, so the three of them really did the *Lear* together, but Guthrie and Casson were absolutely thrown out of the window by the force of Barker's personality, though they did an awful lot of the hard work for him, and it was a great pity that he wasn't completely concentrated on doing it himself, because the actors found him absolutely magical and illuminating.

RYLANDS: Can you just describe what the magic was?

GIELGUD: It was the Toscanini authority mixed with a

curious humanity and an enormous knowledge of the scaf-
folding of the work, not only as a student, as a professor, but
also as a stage manager and a stage director; but as well as
that there was a feeling that he was ready to improvise and
that he summed up your possibilities almost the first day. I
remember him coming to a production of mine of *Hamlet*
before the war and giving me notes. He said, 'Well, Laertes
is no good; we won't discuss him. Now the King is a cat,
you see, and he ought to be a dog' – things like that. It was
so quick, and he had only just made a few notes, and it
immediately gave me a clue about what to say to the actors
afterwards. I found all his notes for *Lear* and I have republished
them[1]; I hope people will be interested to read them, because
the two or three words he said about many lines in the play
were so pithy and clear and such wonderful direction for any
actor, that I think it will be thrilling for people just to read
them in print and see what a really brilliant mind like that can
do. I remember very well in the last scene of *Lear* I said, 'Do
you think I could find the rope that had hanged her in the
soldier's hand at the back of the stage when I'm wandering
around; could this be perhaps effective?' He said, 'Oh no, it's
very Tree. You can't do that. It's like the old-fashioned thing.'
Then, after two days, he suddenly said, 'I rather think that was
a good idea you had about the rope.' This gave me enormous
pleasure because he had somehow woven it into his conception
of the scene. Nothing is more flattering to an actor than when
he invents something and can be allowed to use it with such
authority. When Barker told me anything was good I never
wanted to change it again, whatever the people said from the
front or the critics or anybody who came round. You had this
feeling of absolute confidence in his criticism.

RYLANDS: I suppose you have read all Barker's prefaces?

GIELGUD: Yes indeed. I always enthuse about them whenever I'm doing a production; everybody reads them.

RYLANDS: How much Shakespeare criticism do you normally read, or have you read in your life?

GIELGUD: The man to whom I always go back and whom
I really love, perhaps because I only met him once or twice,
is John Masefield, who wrote short essays.

[1] In *Stage Directions*

RYLANDS: They are brilliant.

GIELGUD: I once went to see him; it was during the war when we were doing *Macbeth*: I wanted advice about it and asked him if he would see me and I went down and had lunch with him. I shall never forget the way he spoke of *Macbeth*, almost as if he had written it himself. He spoke of each line with such love and tenderness and understanding that you really felt he had lived with this play all his life and it was as dear to him as a child; it was extraordinary, it was so wise.

RYLANDS: That Home University Library book of his is about fifty years old.

GIELGUD: He told me he wrote it in three months on a commission from some publishers when he was twenty-six.

RYLANDS: And every single thing in it tells and is so original.

GIELGUD: Oh, so brilliant; and it is easy for actors to read it because it isn't complicated and long-winded, and even the little précis of the plays at the beginning of each one are awfully good.

RYLANDS: What do you think about Shakespeare between the wars, and Shakespeare since 1945 or 1950? Has the old tradition broken, is there a new tradition and is it a good one?

GIELGUD: It's very hard to tell. It seems to me there has been much too much done, since the Vic and Stratford have become established. I suppose I feel a bit jealous of the panoply of the modern Shakespeare set-up in England, because when I was at the Vic at the end of the Twenties it was so exciting to do these plays, not to have the critics come on the first night and sometimes not to have them come at all, to play a thing about thirteen times and to have a production costing £15. It made it such an adventure and such an experiment: you felt you could sort of try your wings and if you fell down a bit they would still forgive you, and if you did succeed it was frightfully exciting. Whereas now the whole standard is much higher. On the other hand, you cannot expect to get more than one good production in three years, because there is too much done and people either fall back on hack work or on gimmicks.

RYLANDS: On the other hand the last twenty years have brought forward plays which have been totally neglected since Shakespeare's time.

GIELGUD: Yes, his less-known plays have certainly come

into their own for the first time, and the young directors like Peter Hall are frightfully interested in doing plays that are not completely smothered in stage tradition because they find that gets in the way both of their actors and of their own ideas about direction.

RYLANDS: And this has altered everybody's feeling about Shakespeare?

GIELGUD: I would say so; and I think the radio has done a tremendous amount to popularise it, people are more familiar with the plays. I mean it was people like Churchill – the old-school Establishment people – who knew their Shakespeare by heart; they say Churchill could go and prompt at Olivier all through *Antony and Cleopatra* which I well believe, because he knew every line.

RYLANDS: He said he learnt all he knew about English history from reading Shakespeare.

GIELGUD: I don't think that people used to know Shakespeare as well as they do now; but now they do hear it on the radio continually and usually see three or four productions a year. And schoolchildren see much more finished productions. I saw the Youth Theatre production of *Julius Caesar*, and I thought that really was a step in a completely fresh direction: it was better than anything I have seen at either university, and it had the most amazing pace and skill. It was not well acted, but it had a marvellous understanding of the text. I understood everything everybody said.

RYLANDS: Pace and clarity are what Barker was very keen on, and what I think has been sacrificed at the present time.

GIELGUD: Of course.

RYLANDS: Do you think that there is now a slight antipathy to poetry as such, a sort of feeling that Shakespeare is poetical and 'may God forgive you for speaking blank verse' – that there is a certain hostility to that as being Victorian?

GIELGUD: Yes, the young actors all want to try to make it more colloquial, but the great danger is that they are inclined to kill the pace by putting in realistic pauses to make it as if they had really thought it at that moment. Instead of which I've always said that if you lie on it, like lying on the water when you are trying to swim, it sustains you, and if you kick about and make holes in the water you go down and drown.

RYLANDS: I don't know whether you remember, some years

ago you gave me a book by Stark Young, that American dramatic critic who died not long ago, which is called *The Flower in Drama; and Glamour* which you said was very good and which absolutely bowled me over. He has in it a chapter entirely about the voice in the theatre, in which he says that in our theatre sound is almost forgotten, that every dramatist has his own voice, every language has its own voice, and an actor's voice is his most important medium, the tone an actor uses can move us more than any other thing about him: our theatres cultivate the eye and not the ear. I think this is absolutely true, and this brings me to your recitals where the eye goes into the background and it is the ear which counts.

GIELGUD: On the other hand I think it is also the Ancient Mariner's beady eye on the audience which holds them there, so that one cannot entirely discard the personal contact of the actor with the audience, which to me is greater in that recital than in any performance I have ever given of Shakespeare; because I play the whole recital to the audience or to myself, but not to other characters. They never lose my face for a single moment and that is one of the reasons why I'm sure it holds so well; and they are so surprised to hear every word. Nearly always in Shakespeare they miss a lot through the movement and through the colour of the costumes and people turning upstage with their backs to them, and so on. And that's why people want the apron stage, and the semi-circular and the rostrum. In a soliloquy you can come near to the audience: I once gave a performance in a sort of senate house in Madras during a monsoon, and the stage was so far back that obviously nobody would hear; so we quickly redirected *Hamlet* in about two hours by having a little stage built over the orchestra pit; and that was to me one of the most thrilling performances I ever played in. The audience was not really on three sides, it was in a semi-circle as in the Sheldonian Theatre, and one was able to get very close to them and look round during a soliloquy and really take their eyes right round the stage and rush off at the side. It was interesting to see how the closeness of the audience seemed to give one much more contact. In the repertory theatre at Birmingham, for instance, which is built on that sort of plan, you get a very good contact and the Mermaid is the same – two of the best modern theatres, merely for the fact that the auditorium is

steeply raked, and when you are far downstage you really
have strong control of the house, more I would say than in a
semi-circular theatre like Chichester, where members of the
audience see one another across the stage, and where the
actors are continually having to turn in order to be seen: that
seems to me very difficult.

RYLANDS: Your Cassius in the *Julius Caesar* film was very
powerful and effective. Did you learn anything about Shakespeare from doing a film?

GIELGUD: Yes, I did to some extent. I'm sure I wouldn't
have played it so well if I hadn't known the part complete.
Brando, who was so brilliant in moments, didn't know the
line of the Forum scene. The director fondly hoped that by
making him do it in tiny bits, he could give the whole effect
of the scene, but as Marlon Brando didn't know the whole
play – didn't know where the climaxes really came in these
speeches – he went in and out and round about and was in
complete confusion; the scene lost its impetus altogether,
because he didn't know where he was going in the part. If
you've played one of those great parts right through, you
know where the beginning and the middle and the end come,
and the same thing with all the speeches. I find that in the
recital I have to be terribly certain where I begin, where I'm
going to and where I'm going to finish, and this thing must
have a line. I think it was Barker who told me, 'You must
have a line of a speech, and inside that line you can have any
number of variations and cadenzas. Don't bother about the
peak moment, don't bother about how you're going to say
"to be or not to be", but worry about everything round it so
that when "to be or not to be" comes you empty your mind
and do it the best way for that particular performance; some
days it will be very good, other days it will fail, but it will
always be of a certain quality, because you've placed it in the
right place.' You must of course have a regular performance
so you won't disappoint the customers but in a great poetic
part you can only hope to reach the heights once or twice,
perhaps, in the whole run, or certainly not more than once
or twice a week, however carefully you plan it and however
successful you are generally in playing it. You've got to hope
that the gods will descend on you.

The *Listener*, 23rd April 1964

DISTINGUISHED COMPANY

23

OVERTURE – BEGINNERS

My first play – *Peter Pan – The Boy Who Wouldn't Grow Up*. I must have been seven years old at least when I saw him first. (Actually he was born the same year that I was, in 1904.) Pauline Chase played Peter, Hilda Trevelyan was Wendy, and Holman Clark was Hook. There was a drop curtain painted to look like a huge sampler, and a mysterious character called Liza who ran across at the beginning and was supposed to have written the play. I was thrilled by the first entrance of the Pirates, drawn on a kind of trolley with Hook enthroned at the centre of the group, and the sinister song that heralded them as they approached from behind the scenes. I loved Nana taking the socks in her mouth from the nursery fender. Was she a real St Bernard, I wondered, or a man dressed up and walking on all fours? But I resented the wires on the children's backs which I could see glittering in the blue limelight, and guessed that their nightgowns had bunched-up material on the shoulders to hide the harness they wore underneath. And I wished the wallpaper at the top of the scenery didn't have to split open, as well as the tall windows, when the time came for them to fly away. Trap doors immediately fascinated me – the one in *Peter Pan*, through which the little house rose slowly at the end of the play, with Peter and Wendy waving to the audience from its windows, and the one in *Where the Rainbow Ends* which suddenly whisked the wicked Aunt and Uncle to the nether regions. And of course I loved the fights in both plays: Peter and Hook, St George and The Dragon King, and the double scene above and below ground in *Peter*, and the hollow tree with stairs inside it, with

Hook in a green limelight leaning over the low door at the bottom, leering at the children as they lay asleep.

I never much cared for pantomimes. The story was always so disjointed, and the Principal Boy who was a girl, the Dame who was a man, and the knockabout comedians and topical songs, made the whole thing very confusing and difficult for me to follow.

These are early memories, of course – childhood treats when my grandmother or my parents always accompanied me. But later in my school days, with a latchkey in my pocket and a few half-crowns carefully saved up from my allowance, I would spend long impatient hours waiting in a queue for the pit or gallery of a theatre, with my brother Val or a schoolfellow for company. After our long hours of waiting we would hear the doors being unbarred at last and would shuffle slowly along in line to pay our money.

In those days the strange method of admission was not by paper ticket but by a metal disc, which was shovelled out from the booking-window after we had paid our shilling or half-crown. Then, clutching our disc, we had to drop it back into the slit of a wooden box a few yards further on before we were finally admitted. We rushed along a dark passage to a flight of steep steps leading down to the pit, or climbed several long flights of stone stairs to reach the gallery. The seats, when we clambered into them at last, were hard wooden benches, sometimes with iron back-rests, sometimes without, so that the knees of the people sitting in the row behind us would press sharply against our shoulders. As we looked down from the gallery the floor of the stage looked absurdly raked, and the actors at the back of a scene were often only visible from the waist downwards, while from the pit our view of the stage was often blocked by tall people sitting in the stalls and by late-comers pushing past them to reach their seats.

In some theatres the underside of the dress circle hung very low, and from the pit the top of the proscenium was cut off completely, and there were often pillars which one had to dodge in order to see the stage at all. If the play was a great success extra rows of stalls would be added and the pit reduced to a few rows at the very back of the theatre, while the second balcony (the 'upper' circle as it was called in those days) was

often enlarged during a successful run, and the gallery pushed
back till it consisted of only a few seats close up against the
roof.

Advertisements, bills, and programmes were designed individually, and I always connected certain colours and typeset-
ting with various managements and their respective theatres.
His Majesty's used buff colour, with red and black print in
very bold readable lettering, and the Haymarket, Wyndham's, and the St James's all had their own particular types
of bills. Then there were boards outside the theatre which
displayed only one name, known, when I learned theatrical
jargon, as 'double-crowns'. On these bills the name of each
star in the play would be printed singly (as well as in lights,
along with the title of the piece, over the main entrance), but
a few of the principal supporting players would also be
featured on individual boards, and when an actor began to be
cast in more important parts he would look forward to the
moment when the management might think him sufficiently
important to merit one all to himself.

Shaftesbury Avenue, Charing Cross Road, and St Martin's
Lane looked much as they do today, though one no longer
sees tramps and down-and-outs sleeping on newspapers in
the alleys at the back of the theatres. But Soho (with its
three-course meals in the little restaurants for a shilling or
two) was still like a discreet foreign village, and the clutter of
cheapjack advertisements, reeking food counters and shoddy
porn shops, were not to disfigure the neighbourhood for
many years to come. Charing Cross Road was filled with
respectable second-hand book shops, and the less discreet
'rubber shops' did not begin till you had passed the Palace
Theatre on your way to the Tottenham Court Road.

The Café Royal was still one of the sights of the West End,
frequented by a crowd of painters and Bohemians. The main
brasserie was approached by a long ramp leading from the
front doors in Regent Street past a big kiosk selling foreign
papers and magazines, and my eldest brother took me there
one day in 1915, when he was on leave, and pointed out
Augustus John holding court, with his earrings, red beard,
and wide black felt hat. On the following afternoon we went
together in a box to the Alhambra to see *The Bing Boys on
Broadway* (arriving, to my dismay, nearly half an hour late

for the performance after a festive lunch party at the Gobelins Restaurant in Rupert Street where I had sat fidgeting and agonisingly looking at my watch). George Robey leaned over the footlights and picked up one of my chocolates, grinning and raising his huge black eyebrows, and Violet Loraine sang one of her songs, as I thought, looking especially in my direction. How did I react, I wonder, to this early experience of audience participation? Fascinated, perhaps, but a bit alarmed as well.

First nights in London used to be such great occasions – at least I thought so. The queues would begin to form outside the theatre several hours earlier than usual, though they behaved in a more orderly fashion than in Victorian days (as my father used to describe them to me) when the men had to move their ladies into the centre of the crush, and protect them by shoving with their elbows in the stampede that always took place as soon as the doors were opened. My father first admired my mother, before he ever met her, when he saw her from the Lyceum pit as she sat with her mother and sisters in a box at one of Irving's first nights.

I came to recognise many of the habitual first-nighters – the critics, including A. B. Walkley of *The Times* and Malcolm Watson of the *Morning Post*, Edward Marsh, with his pointed jutting eyebrows and a monocle, Willie Clarkson, the wig maker, Courtenay Thorpe the actor, with a frilled shirt and false white-gloved hand, quizzing the house through a gold lorgnette, and Mrs Aria, who had been Irving's last devoted friend and was a famous wit. ('In all matters pertaining to Sir Henry,' she once observed to a young lady who repeated some indiscreet gossip at a party, 'I believe I am considered to be the past-mistress.') Various leading actors and actresses – one of the Vanbrugh sisters perhaps, Marie Tempest, or even Ellen Terry, were quickly recognised as they entered the stalls or boxes (they timed their appearances with care so as not to divide the interest of the pit and gallery) and would be greeted with excited cries and enthusiastic applause which they would acknowledge gracefully, bowing to the audience as they took their seats. The curtain would rise at least ten minutes late, and there would be more excitement as the scenery (also applauded if it was at all spectacular) was disclosed, and more clapping as each of the principal actors made their entrance. In the intervals I looked forward to the buzz of argument and comment in the foyer and, at the end of the performance, the shouts of approval (or perhaps booing) from the gallery, and speeches from the star, the director (dragged on and usually ineptly inaudible) and sometimes from the author (whom the audience often failed to recognise). Then, after it was all over, the long journey back to South Kensington by tube or bus, dead tired but still arguing excitably all the way.

CHU CHIN CHOW

1916, and His Majesty's Theatre packed with uniforms. I am twelve years old, sitting with my parents in my favourite seat, the middle of the front row of the Dress Circle. The lights go slowly down and music plays. Clouds of delicious incense are wafted from the stage as the gold fringed red velvet curtain rises on a dazzling palace scene, a dark blue banqueting hall with marble steps and a frieze of peacocks that looks like beaten gold. Negro slaves, led by a major domo in a huge turban carrying a wand, parade with covered dishes. 'Here be oysters stewed in honey', they sing, 'all for our great Lord Kassim.' Oscar Asche makes his entrance, huge and impressive, with long moustaches and gilded fingernails, rattling his Chinese fan, and Lily Brayton, his wife, in a great wig of frizzed black hair, swathed in veils and jewels and transparent gauzes.

Courtice Pounds as Ali Baba singing (with Aileen D'Orme) the hit song of the evening 'Any Time's Kissing Time'. Sydney Fairbrother[1] as Ali Baba's comic wife Mahbubah. Frank Cochrane, as Kassim Baba, murdered in a cave full of jewels at the end of the second act, reappears in the part of a blind cobbler in the third. 'And as I cobble with needle and thread, I judge the world by the way they tread.' There are two real donkeys, several goats, some sheep, and at

---

[1] A brilliant eccentric actress – she was apt at rehearsal to produce live mice from her sleeves or bosom – adored dogs – and wore very strange clothes. 'Don't care for jewellery, dear,' she said to me once – 'Beads can't resist them!'

least one camel. The next time I come to see the play again – I shall see it nearly a dozen times – I shall have the added pleasure of watching the animals arriving at the stage-door as I stand waiting in the long queue, listening to the buskers and exchanging theatre gossip with my neighbours.

Chu Chin Chow ran for years, but it always seemed fresh and fascinating to me, even when a dreaded slip in the programme would announce that one of my favourite players was ill or taking a holiday. But the lighting and scenery appeared as beautiful as ever, and a bill announcing 'New scenes, New songs, New costumes', issued after two years' run, sent me scurrying off to His Majesty's once more. The piece was nothing in itself, simply the old fairy tale of *Ali Baba and the Forty Thieves*, but Asche had made it into a brilliant fantasy, part pantomime, part romance, part musical comedy, and had also written the book with the composer Frederic Norton, whose music was so charming and so hugely popular. Black velvet Moorish shutters (a kind of false proscenium) slid together at the end of each full scene, and opened to reveal insets on little rostrums where duets were sung while another full scene was prepared behind, an infinitely more attractive solution than the flapping front cloths which had always been accepted before this time in plays demanding elaborate scenery.

Besides an excellent cast of players and a most convincing group of extras drilled to perfection, Asche had taken care to engage a number of beautiful girls, whom he deployed in the slave-market scene wearing spectacular and scanty costumes, a kind of London version of the Folies Bergères. This episode was naturally one of the production's most popular features, especially to the men on leave who crowded the theatre. Sir Herbert Tree, who had built His Majesty's, returned from America, where he had gone to recoup some past failures, to find his 'Beautiful Theatre' packed to the doors with *Chu Chin Chow* and sat among the audience murmuring sadly, 'More navel than millinery.'

It was in the same year that I saw the revue, *Vanity Fair*, produced by Alfred Butt at the Palace Theatre. The opening scene was set in Piccadilly Circus, and Arthur Playfair and Nelson Keys, two brilliant comedians, acted in a hilarious skit called 'Two-chinned-chow' – Playfair imitating Oscar Asche, while Nelson Keys, in an enormous fuzzy wig, with bare legs, his arms covered with bracelets and hands spread out with palms downwards in Cleopatra style, ran coyly round the Eros fountain, his body swathed in black wrappings with two large yellow hands embroidered on them, appearing to clasp him round the waist. He gave a brilliant caricature of Lily Brayton's way of talking in the play, with a lot of pseudo-Oriental jabber, and the scene ended with the Forty Thieves entering from the back of the stage, carrying on their shoulders the sandwich-boards which were commonly used to advertise plays in the streets in those days. The boards were printed in large letters in the colour and type of the posters for His Majesty's, and read, 'Stalls Full', 'Dress Circle Full', 'Gallery Full', 'Awfull'.

SHAKESPEARE TERCENTENARY PERFORMANCE 2 MAY 1916

Drury Lane Theatre, a gala matinée

My brother Val and I sit with our parents, in the Upper Circle this time, as seats for such a grand occasion are very expensive. King George and Queen Mary arrive in the Royal Box and the whole audience rises to greet them. Sir George Alexander has arranged the performance, as Tree (considered to be the leader of the Profession) is still in America. The programme is a formidably long one, nearly half an hour of orchestral pieces and some solos by various eminent singers, followed by the whole of Shakespeare's *Julius Caesar*, and a pageant to finish up with, as well as speeches from Sir Squire Bancroft and Mrs Kendal. But of course we sit spellbound from beginning to end. The Forum scene is magnificently played, with a great crowd of distinguished citizens led by Gerald du Maurier and Edmund Gwenn. We quickly decide that Henry Ainley, stripped to a leopard skin for the games in the opening scene, is an ideal Mark Antony, and Arthur Bourchier a rather dull and heavy Brutus. Also that Cassius, superbly played by H. B. Irving, is the best part in the play, an opinion from which I have never wavered since. The Alma-Tadema scenery, designed for Tree's production at His Majesty's years before, is used again, with solid-looking palaces, balconies and awnings, pillars, perspectives, and blue skies.

During one of the intervals we hear a great outburst of cheering from behind the curtain, and someone comes out to tell us that Frank Benson, who is playing Caesar, has just been sent for to the Royal Box, still in his corpse-like make-up as the Ghost, to be knighted by the King with a sword hastily borrowed from Simmonds, the theatrical costumier's round the corner in King Street. The audience cheer wildly at the announcement, taking up the applause from the huge crowd of delighted players behind the scenes.

The great pantomime was still being presented every year at Drury Lane by Arthur Collins, an experienced master of such productions, and the previous Christmas he had used a massive pillared set for the finale – wide steps stretching from under the stage close to the footlights from the open trap, rising to the very top of the huge stage, with two broad landings to divide the ascending flights of stairs. The same set is used again for the Shakespearean pageant this May afternoon. Groups of characters from nine or ten of the plays emerge in procession, coming up from below with their backs towards the audience. On reaching the landings they turn and reveal themselves – Ellen and Marion Terry as Portia and Nerissa, Fred Terry and Julia Neilson as Benedick and Beatrice, and dozens more. Every star of the legitimate and musical stage in London at the time is recognised and greeted by the enraptured house. The clapping never seems to stop. When all the players in the various tableaux have been applauded and have stepped aside, curtains on the top landing are drawn back, revealing a bust of Shakespeare on a plinth. Flanking the bust are the figures of Comedy and Tragedy – Ellen Terry in white and Geneviève Ward in black – and the huge cast of players begin to move slowly up the last flight of stairs to lay wreaths at the foot of the plinth. Finally with the singing of the National Anthem, the curtain falls and the performance is over.

Percy Macquoid, the great furniture and costume expert, who was also an experienced man of the theatre and had helped

Tree and Alexander in many of their finest productions, was a great friend of my parents. He told us afterwards some funny stories of the great occasion. How Evelyn Millard, who played Calpurnia, begged, 'Oh, Mr Macquoid, couldn't I have a different togo?' and that Bourchier, when Macquoid remonstrated with him for wearing white socks with his sandals, looked very cross and demanded, 'Ain't they right, old boy?' Geneviève Ward (who had played Queen Eleanor in *Becket* at the Lyceum with Henry Irving) was evidently something of a terror, and had made a fuss at being asked to share a dressing-room with a number of other distinguished actresses, not having bothered to read the imposing list of names pinned to the door. Ellen Terry, who was already in the room, making up quietly in a corner, was heard to murmur softly, 'You always were a cat, Ginny!'

Miss Ward was however a fine tragedienne, a famous Volumnia in *Coriolanus*, a part she often played with Benson's company, and the first actress to be made a Dame. But Ellen Terry was not similarly honoured till several years later, presumably because of her marital irregularities, and the title only came to her when she was too old to take much pleasure from it. The whole theatrical profession was deeply indignant that she had not been the first actress to be singled out. As the two actresses stood opposite to one another at Drury Lane that afternoon, I remember watching Ellen Terry, as she held the mask of Comedy for many minutes in her outstretched hand, restlessly dropping it to her side from time to time, while Geneviève Ward stood like the Rock of Gibraltar, holding her Tragic mask with a grip of steel.

24

FAMILY PORTRAIT

FRED, MARION, AND DAME ELLEN TERRY

'Ladies and gentlemen. If there is anything an actor values more than your applause, it is your silent attention to detail which enables us to give you of our best. On behalf of my dear comrade Julia Neilson and all the comrades of my company, I thank you from my heart.' This was one of Fred Terry's characteristic curtain speeches.

He was an imposing figure, my great-uncle, when I first became aware of him at my parents' Christmas parties, built on generous lines, with fine hands and red curly hair. Extremely shortsighted, and wearing gold pince-nez like his master, Henry Irving, he behaved, as he acted, in the grand manner, jingling the sovereigns in the pockets of his striped grey trousers – worn with a black stock, tailcoat, and button boots – the typical Edwardian actor-manager.

He loved his work with a dedicated devotion, and was touchingly sincere and simple in his attitude towards it. For him heroes and heroines were always white and villains always black. A faithful disciple of Irving, Tree, and Alexander, in whose companies he had so often appeared in his first years as a young actor, he followed their example by embellishing his own productions with fine scenery and lavish costumes, and drilled his crowds and ensemble scenes with loving care, perfecting elaborately worked-up entrances and effective 'curtains' and using music to give background to dramatic or sentimental scenes. Max Beerbohm, writing of his performance in a drama entitled *Dorothy o' The Hall*

(in which Dorothy Vernon danced with Queen Elizabeth),
remarked, 'Mr Terry . . . hiding behind a bower of roses,
thrust his face through the flowers, in sight of the audience,
without seeming ridiculous. Mr Terry thrusts his face thus
and stays thus, for several seconds: and yet manages to remain,
as he would say, "mahnly". It is a remarkable achievement.'

Jolly, warm and generous, he was also a man of violent
prejudices, and subject to sudden and violent fits of apoplectic
rage which quickly passed like clouds before the sun. His
language could be sulphurous, though he managed to restrain
it in front of ladies, to whom he was always extremely
courteous. He was fond of gambling, and would spend long
hours playing bridge at one of his London clubs (he was a
great clubman) or swearing furiously if he played badly on
the golf course or backed a loser on the race-course. On one
occasion, feeling it was necessary to call a young actor to
order for using bad language in the Green Room Club, he
sent for the young man in question and spoke to him severely.
'Well,' said the culprit, 'I seem to remember, Sir, that I have
sometimes heard you use fairly strong language in the Club
yourself.' 'God all bloody mighty,' retorted Fred Terry, 'I'm
the f . . . President.'

He believed completely in the romantic nonsense in which
he acted so successfully, but in modern clothes he knew he
could not achieve the splendid panache which so delighted
his audiences when he was in period costume. He knew
just how to swing a cape, flourish a feathered hat, sweep a
magnificent bow, dance a minuet, spit his opponent with a
flash of his rapier, or light up a commonplace scene with his
lively presence and ringing laugh. But he thought Ibsen
decadent and Shaw discursive. Clean, full-blooded romantic
melodrama was his acknowledged field, and he revelled in it
all through his theatre life, and occasionally in his private life
as well.

Marion, his favourite sister, who acted so delightfully in
plays by Wilde and Barrie, had also been beautifully trained
in Shakespeare and costume plays. She too was somewhat
narrow in her outlook and lacked humour in private life,
where she demanded a good deal of flattery and attention.
But she was a brilliant actress, shrewd enough to adapt her
technique to a more realistic manner as time went by, even

succeeding (as Lilian Braithwaite, who had often worked with her, when she herself was an *ingénue*, was also to do in *The Vortex* some twenty years later) as 'the woman with the past', when she created the part of the adventuress, Mrs Erlynne, in Wilde's *Lady Windermere's Fan*. Her last appearance in London was in Somerset Maugham's *Our Betters*, as the Princess, one of the only two respectable characters in the comedy, which was considered at that time (1923) to be extremely daring, and I always wondered what Marion herself must have thought of the play when she agreed to act in it. Fred would most certainly have disapproved of it profoundly.

It is sad that Ellen Terry, the greatest and most famous of the Terry family, could not succeed in finding vehicles for her talent after leaving the Lyceum, whereas her sister and brother – Fred was the youngest of the family – continued to appear in London and the provinces right up to the Twenties. Ellen was to triumph only once more for a season at His Majesty's as Mistress Page with Tree (though Irving was still alive), in his Coronation production of *The Merry Wives of Windsor* in 1902. In this she appeared with Mrs Kendal, her life-long rival and, according to my father, the best actress in England, though never to be compared in popularity with Ellen Terry. In 1905 Tree also presented *The Winter's Tale* for Ellen at his theatre though he did not himself appear in it (Charles Warner was Leontes), but she seems not to have made any great impression as Hermione. Her memory, as with all the Terrys, was treacherously uncertain, and her concentration easily disturbed, though she continued to the end of her life to enchant the public whenever they were lucky enough to see her on or off the stage.

Ellen Terry drew her characters, with instinctive genius, in broad strokes and generous flowing lines, but she seemed too restless to be confined within the walls of drawing-room comedy or even in contemporary heroic drama. Her failure as Hiordis in Ibsen's *The Vikings* (which she daringly produced in 1903 under her own management chiefly to display the scenic talents of her son Gordon Craig) must have made her wary of venturing into more experimental work. She had listened too late to Shaw's entreaties, and stayed too long at the Lyceum, with its fading fortunes, out of a strong sense of professional discipline and unwillingness to dissolve her long and triumphant partnership with Irving.

She could not help loving to be loved, and, as the public always preferred her to make them laugh or cry (they would have none of her as a tragedienne, either as Lady Macbeth or Volumnia), she went on playing Goldsmith's Olivia and Nance Oldfield,[1] with Portia and Katharine of Aragon to bring her back to her beloved Shakespeare from time to time, so long as the passing years allowed. In her seventies, when I heard her give her Shakespeare lecture readings, she could still give radiant glimpses of her former glory, and one could understand the older generation of playgoers who said, 'She speaks Shakespeare as if she had just been talking to him in the next room.' But the only two contemporary plays in which she appeared at the turn of the century, Barrie's *Alice Sit By The Fire* (1905) and Shaw's *Captain Brassbound's Conversion* (1906), proved something of a disappointment, and her divine gifts of tears and sunshine never seemed to inspire a new playwright to provide her with adequate material.

I think both Fred and Marion were always somewhat afraid of their elder sister, perhaps because she was apt to be slyly amused at their immense seriousness and respectability, and was basically far simpler and more unashamedly Bohemian than they were. When she was engaged by Doris Keane in 1919 to play the Nurse in *Romeo and Juliet* – her last professional appearance in a London run – she wrote with glee, 'I am keeping all the rude bits in!' – a remark which would certainly have shocked her brother and sister. But perhaps the shade of Irving would have chuckled. Himself a somewhat bitter and ironic humorist, he had never been able to resist her enormous sense of fun, even when she arrived late for rehearsals and broke up the other actors by fooling during a performance, behaviour which he would never have countenanced from anyone else within the sacred portals of his theatre.

All the Terrys had healthy appetites, enormous courage, and staying-power – especially in honouring their acting

---

[1] *Olivia* by Wills adapted from *The Vicar of Wakefield*. *Nance Oldfield*, a one-act play by Charles Reade.

commitments – poor eyesight, bad memories, and intermittently indifferent health. They all possessed expressive hands – Fred's were beautiful (but Ellen's were not, though she used them wonderfully), and they all contrived to move with unfailing grace. Marion took the stage with immense distinction, even when bowed with age (there was a sensational moment one Christmas, when my mother warned us that Aunt Marion's hair was white and we must not appear to notice; she had always dyed it red which of course we had not realised), while Ellen appeared to dart across the scene, giving an impression of dragonfly swiftness and outdoor freedom. 'But look where Beatrice, like a lapwing, runs close by the ground to hear our conference.' Even when I saw her at the Coliseum and another time at a theatre on the West Pier at Brighton, during the First World War, acting the Trial Scene of *The Merchant of Venice* and some scenes as Mistress Page (with a young Edith Evans as Nerissa and Mistress Ford), she seemed to bring a breath of fresh air with her the moment she stepped on to the stage.

Ellen, Marion, and Fred – all three spoke with unerring diction, phrasing, and flow of thought, in the melting beauty of their inimitable Terry voices. As one can see from Ellen's rehearsal-scripts, she would rewrite and rephrase her lines as she tried to memorise them, in order to make them sound spontaneous and more natural, managing to breathe life into the stilted speeches allotted to her, even in fustian plays like *The Dead Heart* and *Ravenswood*, the later Irving productions at the Lyceum. Irving himself had always used the same method with his most famous parts (in his melodramas, *The Bells*, and *Louis XI* for instance), and Fred used to follow the same example, cutting and adding continually over many performances to build up the effects he needed, though of course this was an impossible method to use in Shakespeare or in a really well-written modern play.

Fred could add grace to the most commonplace lines. As he leaned over the back of the garden seat in the scene at Richmond in *The Scarlet Pimpernel* and said to Lady Blakeney 'Madam, will you not dry those tears? I could never bear to see a pretty woman cry,' he would suddenly lower his voice a whole octave and a hush would spread over the entire audience.

Lady Tree, 1935

Mrs Patrick Campbell, 1913

Viola Tree, C.B. Cochran, Sacha Guitry and Yvonne Printemps

Cedric Hardwicke and Gwen Ffrangcon-
Davies in *The Barretts of Wimpole Street* at
the Queen's Theatre, 1930

Charles Hawtrey in *Ambrose Applejohn's
Adventure* at the Criterion Theatre, 1921

Toni Edgar Bruce, Lottie Venne, Leon Quartermaine, Allan Aynesworth and E.
Holman Clark standing in *The Circle* at the Theatre Royal, Haymarket, 1921

Squire Bancroft, 1883

Willie Clarkson, 1929

W. Graham Robertson by John
Singer Sargent

Lillah McCarthy and Matheson Lang
at the New Theatre, 1920

Violet Vanbrugh as Lady Macbeth,
1912

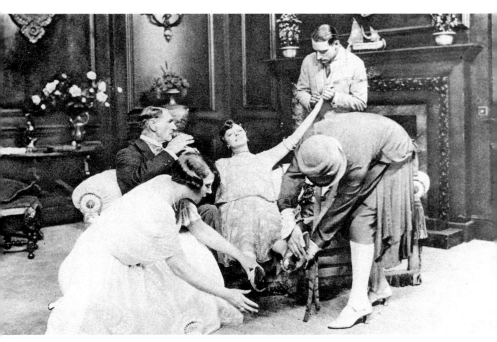

Aubrey Smith, Marie Löhr, Irene Vanbrugh and Henry Daniel
in *Caroline* by Somerset Maugham

He loved to help young people if he possibly could, with money, encouragement, and good advice. He once sent for a young actor whom I knew and advised him to leave his company to take an engagement in the West End (this was towards the end of his own career, when he was touring with cheaper actors than before). He told the boy that he was ready to better himself and could learn no more from him. He helped to train the young Donald Wolfit, who always acknowledged all he had learned from him. When he was not acting himself he would go to see the current successes in the London theatres, standing at the back of the pit so that he could slip in and out unnoticed. He once engaged his nephew Gordon Craig to design a scene for him, though I doubt if he really understood his work. But he could never bring himself to appear in plays that he could not pretend to like and, in spite of recurring ill-health which he resisted with the greatest courage, he remained in management with his wife, acting in the vehicles they had always loved and in which they felt they both showed to the best advantage. They continued to give regular seasons in London with varying success, and managed to recover the losses of their occasional failures by touring the big provincial cities, where their arrivals and departures were always something of a royal progress.

Of course Fred should have played Falstaff in his later years, and he would have been a magnificent Sir Peter Teazle. But he preferred to act Benedick, for which he was then too old, and Bothwell and Henry the Eighth in two indifferent melodramas, probably because they gave equal opportunities to his wife. He had appeared as Charles Surface in his young days, and told me that once, acting in the Screen Scene with the famous old actor William Farren as Sir Peter, Mrs Patrick Campbell, hidden behind the screen as Lady Teazle, became exasperated by their slowness, and boomed out, 'Oh, do get on, you old pongers!' Someone congratulated him on the way he flicked his lace handkerchief over his uncle's portrait in the auction scene, but Fred only said modestly, 'Ah, that's Coghlan's business.' It was always touching to hear the respect and admiration he expressed for Irving and his famous predecessors of the past.

When he first produced *The Scarlet Pimpernel* in the

provinces, it was not much liked, and Fred realised instinctively that as nearly all the action took place offstage, a more lively scene to open the play might get it off to a better start. So a prologue was introduced, set at one of the Gates of Paris, with the Pimpernel, disguised as an old woman, driving a ramshackle cart in which, of course, the aristocrats he was saving from The Terror were concealed. The new opening proved an enormous success and the play was to stand him in good stead for twenty years and more. As soon as it became talked about, everyone got to know that the hag in the Paris scene was Blakeney, despite his disguise of a false nose and shabby bonnet, and the entrance of the cart (drawn by a real horse – ever a hazardous but popular addition to any drama in those days) always drew a round of applause to greet the star. But Fred soon decided that he need not trouble to add to his labours by the task of making a quick change of clothes and make-up so early in the evening, and after a few weeks preferred to entrust the part of the old hag to his obedient understudy. Of course the audience were unaware of the deception and applauded just the same. But Fred instructed his dresser to stand in the wings at every performance and solemnly hand the Terry pince-nez to the understudy as he dismounted from the cart. It is not recorded whether the company were deceived by this charming little trick.

Fred's historical romances were always strictly wholesome, even at the expense of authenticity. Lady Castlemaine and the Duchess of Portsmouth were only malicious ladies at the court of the Merry Monarch, Nell Gwynne herself merely the King's great-hearted friend, who foiled the wicked Judge Jeffreys by dressing up in his wig and gown, making great comic play as she wielded a scratching quill pen and sneezed loudly after taking huge pinches of snuff. At the end of this scene she was triumphantly carried from the stage in a sedan-chair, waving her huge cartwheel feathered hat out of the window. She danced with two of her former actor cronies, accompanied herself on a spinet, and in the last act rushed breathlessly up a staircase from below in a magnificent dress which billowed round her, crying, 'The Queen is too ill to see me. What's to be done?' The part of King Charles, with his real spaniels, was something of a holiday for Fred, but he wore a splendid make-up and played it to perfection, even when one of the dogs bit off the end of his false nose and jumped off his knee to vanish with it through the stage fireplace, to the audience's great delight.

He once mounted a production of *Romeo and Juliet* for his daughter Phyllis. He had intended to act Mercutio, but became ill during rehearsals and finally directed the play without appearing in it himself. A shy young actor, engaged to play the part of Paris, was given an elaborate Carpaccio costume to wear – parti-coloured tights and an Italianate wig falling to his shoulders. Some of the older members of the company, with whom he shared a dressing-room, mischievously drew attention to the inadequacy of his make-up, and finally persuaded him to add mascara to his eyelashes, rouge to his lips, and a dangling pearl to his right ear. Deeply self-conscious in all this finery, the young man slunk timidly on to the stage at the dress parade and bashfully announced himself. Fred, who was asleep in the darkness of the stalls, woke suddenly, rammed his glasses on to his nose, and, roaring with laughter, shouted out, 'My God, it's a tart I once slept with in Bury St Edmunds!'

At the old Borough Theatre, Stratford (long since torn down), on a foggy afternoon after a matinée, he came to the stage door, still dressed in his Pimpernel costume, to press a gold sovereign into my schoolboy hand. On another day he gave me a rich lunch at his Club, and afterwards climbed many flights of stairs in my parents' house to look at my model theatre and the clumsy scenery which I had painted to embellish it. Later, when his daughter had generously given me my first professional engagement, and afterwards, when I had arrived at some success, he never failed to encourage me and write me delightful letters. In one of them he praised my Hamlet, to my great delight, comparing it to that of Irving and Forbes-Robertson and the other great ones who had played the part. And though he professed to be deeply shocked by *The Constant Nymph* (with its Gordon Craig-like character of the Bohemian Sanger, with his mistress and brood of illegitimate children) when he saw it in 1926, he seemed strangely tolerant of an equally ambiguous atmosphere when he came to see me act in Ronald MacKenzie's *Musical Chairs* in 1931. But by that year he had aged considerably, mellowing as his time grew short.

Narrow but generous, simple, direct, and deeply honest –
a 'prince of good fellows' (as he once called the Prince of
Wales at a Public Dinner, only to find his Royal Highness
furtively picking his nose as he sat beside him in the place of
honour) he was a noble figure of the theatre, a consummate
romantic actor, and a great gentleman besides.

TO ACT A NEW PART

The life of Ellen Terry has already been recorded in a number
of vivid and informative memoirs – notably her Autobiography, first published in 1908, and reissued in 1933, with
notes and a record of her later years (she died in 1928) by her
daughter Edith Craig, in collaboration with Christopher St
John, who had worked as 'literary henchman' on the original
memoir and was a close friend of both mother and daughter.
Naturally Mr Manvell, in his new life of the great actress,[1]
has drawn extensively on these two books, as well as quoting
freely from the Shaw-Terry correspondence, the letters and
diaries of Graham Robertson, the two Irving and Terry books
of Gordon Craig, the fine biography of Henry Irving by his
grandson Laurence, Marguerite Steen's *A Pride of Terrys* and
my own mother's autobiography. He has been extremely
adroit in compressing and sorting this mass of relevant detail
into a highly readable and straightforward account, and has
added interest to it by shedding fresh light on many of the
episodes which were suppressed or glossed over in the earlier
books in order to avoid giving offence to surviving personalities or their families in the tactful conventions of the time.

The new book is greatly enriched by admirable sketches of
Frederick Watts, Charles Kelly and James Carew (the three
husbands of Ellen Terry); of her lover, the father of her two
children and great love of her life, Edward Godwin (the
architect and decorator); and of the great Henry Irving, her
partner for so many years of splendour and success at the
Lyceum Theatre. Mr Manvell sides with Laurence Irving (and
against Marguerite Steen) on conjecturing that Irving and
Ellen were never lovers. This is a fascinating riddle, still

[1] *Ellen Terry* by Roger Manvell. Heinemann 1968.

unsolved. Even members of Ellen's family – my own mother and Gordon Craig especially – defiantly rejected it all their lives, though there are two letters from Irving in Mr Manvell's book which I should have thought clinched the certainty of a love affair, during a few years or months at least, of their early partnership in the theatre.

The strictures of Henry James on both Irving's and Ellen Terry's acting talents create an admirable critical balance for readers of today, and show that, amongst the almost unanimous public adulation accorded them both for so many years, they were not without their detractors among a number of discerning playgoers. I find a certain coldness in the book which may largely be accounted for by the fact that, because of my own relationship to Ellen Terry, my lifelong pride in her achievements and my own personal remembrances of her magical charm and humour (even though I only knew her in old age when I was still a schoolboy), have given me a sense of affinity with her that has made me feel that no one could understand her character and talents quite as well as I do.

Gordon Craig, her son (whom I began to know only when I was middle-aged and he was an old man) had a marvellous sense of humour – a rather wicked and yet childishly attractive kind of fun and defiance – which reminded me strongly of his mother as I remember her, though in his case this was allied to a certain malice which I do not at all connect with her, and which seems to me more likely to have come from Godwin, the father whom he knew so little, and idolised yet resented, I fancy, all his life. (Shaw once said cleverly that Craig never quite forgave his mother that Irving was not his father.) Ellen's best known sister and brother, Marion and Fred Terry, were both fine players and enchanting personalities (the one stingy, the other extravagantly generous), both Philistines, somewhat snobbish, typical late Victorians in their outlook, tastes and prejudices. But Ellen was magnificently impulsive, wise (except for her own emotional recklessness), a simple, honest woman – Bohemian and great lady at the same time, she could move in any direction that once engaged her intelligence and common sense. One felt immediately that she had a modern point of view, a desire to understand new people and new trends.

It was only sad that her faculties began to fail her in her

last years, making her dependent on people who guarded her
of necessity, but also troubled her by that possessiveness
and jealousy which so often surrounds a uniquely magnetic
personality. She had always been fond of the company of
men. They stimulated and delighted her, and in old age she
was always hemmed in by women. I cannot resist quoting
from a superb essay, written for the *New Statesman* in 1941
by Virginia Woolf, which I have always kept in my own
copy of Ellen's biography (which she gave me herself in
1917), for it seems so extraordinary perceptive:

> Which then, of all these women is the real Ellen Terry?
> . . . Is she mother, wife, cook, critic, actress, or should she
> have been after all, a painter? Each part seems the right part
> until she throws it aside and paints another . . . Shakespeare
> could not fit her; nor the nursery. But there is, after all, a
> greater dramatist than Shakespeare, Ibsen, or Shaw. There
> is Nature. Hers is so vast a stage, and so innumerable a
> company of actors, that for the most part she fobs them
> off with a tag or two. They come on and they go off
> without breaking the ranks. But now and then Nature
> creates a new part, an original part. The actors who act that
> part always defy our attempts to name them. They will
> not act the stock parts – they forget the words, they
> improvise others of their own. But when they come on,
> the stage falls like a pack of cards and the limelights are
> extinguished. That was Ellen Terry's fate – to act a new
> part – and while other actors are remembered because
> they were Hamlet, Phèdre, or Cleopatra, Ellen Terry is
> remembered because she was Ellen Terry.
>
> *New Statesman*, 12th April 1968

25

BROTHER AND SISTER

EDWARD AND EDITH GORDON CRAIG

Edward and Edith Gordon Craig, the children of Ellen Terry by Edward Godwin, the architect and designer to whom she was never married, were a fascinating pair. The boy was something of a genius – a promising actor who became dissatisfied with acting, and became a brilliant designer, scene-inventor, etcher, woodcutter, and an accomplished and original writer; the girl, equally frustrated, was also an actress *manquée*, handsome, though less physically attractive, and gifted, like her brother, with considerable talents for which she failed, on the whole, to gain the recognition she deserved.

They were both devoted to their mother, but resented the absence of the father whom they had hardly known. Ellen's second husband, Charles Kelly, and afterwards Henry Irving, became substitute father-figures to them both, but they were difficult children to manage and were to cause their mother continual anxiety as they grew older, even though her growing success and popularity, and the large salary which she earned at the Lyceum, enabled her to lavish much care and money on their education. She was inclined to spoil them, though she tried to be very strict. Ted escaped from home and married young, after a turbulent career at various schools and a long restless apprenticeship at the Lyceum, but Edy remained in her mother's house, failing to achieve an early ambition to become a professional pianist through a rheumatic condition which developed when she was studying in Germany.

Ellen Terry, remembering no doubt the failure of her own marriages (the first, to the painter Watts, had been contracted and dissolved when she was little more than a girl), is said to have interfered on two occasions when Edy fell in love. A clique of women friends who flattered and adored her gradually began to influence her strongly, and were apt to involve her mother (whom they also adored) in jealous intrigues and possessiveness. Ted never lived in England after his early years, and, though Ellen loved him devotedly and treasured his occasional visits, she had mostly to be content with paying his debts, sympathising with the various women with whom he was associated at different times, and housing his children when he appeared to be too busy to look after them himself.

The brother and sister were basically very fond of one another, but when they had worked together, under their mother's management, at the Imperial Theatre in 1903, Ted designing and directing and Edy in charge of the costume department, they had failed to get on for various reasons, and Ted soon escaped abroad after the season had proved a disastrous financial failure. Though many had admired and praised the ideas which he conceived in the few productions he had actually carried out in London, he was obviously much before his time, and it was sad that no management had sufficient faith to engage him, as he was reputed to spend money extravagantly and demand to be given complete authority in any theatre in which he worked.

Ted and Edy had both appeared in minor parts with Irving and their mother at the Lyceum. Both became devoted to him, though the experience did not seem to give them great confidence in their own abilities as actors. Surprisingly for that strict time, they were accepted everywhere in society for Ellen Terry's sake, but there is no doubt that the slur of their illegitimacy, as well as a favouritism which they resented, helped to disturb their youthful development.

Edy was not aggressively masculine in personality, though she was sometimes brusque and rude, and very autocratic in dealing with those who worked with her. She was a very clever costume designer, and later an original stage director, but in her best years she was evidently too managing to be tactful or popular. Living in the shadow of Ellen Terry's overwhelming charm, she probably developed a complex about being considerably less attractive than her mother. She had a slight lisp which was hard for her to overcome, and she earned the reputation, as she grew older, of being a kind of dragon, apt to exploit her mother, bullying her, sometimes in front of other people, and forcing her to go on appearing in the theatre when her memory and eyesight were too weak to allow her to shine with her former lustre. Chris Marshall (who changed her name to Christopher St John when she was converted to Catholicism) was Edy's greatest friend, and as devoted to the mother as she was to the daughter. She was the 'literary henchman' who collaborated with Ellen in the writing of her splendid autobiography in 1906, the time of Ellen Terry's Jubilee. After Ellen died in 1928, she and Clare Atwood, the painter, helped Edy with devoted pains to perpetuate her memory, arranging Ellen's Smallhythe Farm as a beautiful museum, and adapting the old Barn which stands in her garden as a small theatre where they organised a matinée every year on the anniversary of her death. Christopher St John also revised Ellen's first book of memoirs and annotated it admirably, while Edy, despite bitter recriminations from her brother (who retorted with a book *Ellen Terry and Her Secret Self* giving his own account of his relationship with his mother), persuaded Bernard Shaw to let her publish the fascinating correspondence between himself and Ellen Terry, which had originated when Shaw was a musical critic and Ellen was still leading lady at the Lyceum.

Edy was as industrious as her brother, and continued working almost till her death, producing plays in churches and pageants in parks and gardens. To me she was always most sympathetic and kindly, a picturesque figure whether in her country smock or rather striking bohemian clothes, delivering her views with brisk authority. In old age she grew to look very like her mother. Many theatre people admired and respected her, though they were somewhat wary of allowing her too much rein for fear of upsetting her collaborators. She was unlucky to have lived at a time when women were not greatly trusted with leading positions in the world of the theatre (except as actresses) and in consequence she always had a good deal of suspicious resentment to contend with. Her mother became fretful and forgetful, and it was necessary for Edy to take every care of her. Her family resented this as an intrusion and criticised her accordingly, but there is no doubt that Ellen and Edy loved each other to the end, in spite of many difficulties and heart-burnings on both sides, fanned by the interference of well-meaning relations, as well as by enemies and devotees.

I appeared under Edy's direction for the first time at a matinée to help some Children's Charity at Daly's Theatre in the early Twenties. There were tableaux of famous Saints (Gladys Cooper as St George, Sybil Thorndike as St Joan) with groups of small children, dressed as cherubs and angels, in the main feature of the programme, a Nativity Play. The Virgin was to be played by Fay Compton, and I was asked to be one of the three shepherds. We had, I think, only one rehearsal, the usual half-baked muddle in some bleak room or other, with half the cast failing to put in an appearance. My own few lines were, I was told, to be spoken as the shepherds walked from the footlights across the stalls on a gangplank stretching to the back of the theatre. We had to sit down near the footlights, munch some food we had with us, and then see the Star in the East and move through the auditorium towards where it was supposed to be.

On the afternoon of the performance the house was not very full. In fact there seemed to be more people on the stage and behind the scenes than in the audience. The mothers of the children who were appearing kept rushing from their seats in the stalls, pushing through the pass door into the wings to attend to their offsprings' manifold emergencies. Stage-hands were trying to find their way among the crowd of actors and actresses who were greeting one another in loud stage whispers. Two huge wolfhounds were held on leashes by Esmé Percy, who was Herod, and George Hayes, his decadent son. Edith Craig herself, with her devoted friends, Christopher St John and Clare Atwood, dressed in voluminous monks' robes, were issuing orders in all directions. As the afternoon wore on and a number of mistakes began to occur, they drew their hoods over their heads and pressed their way on to the stage among the performers. I entered with my two companions, and we proceeded towards the footlights, where we sat to begin our speeches, to find, to our dismay, that slices of delicious soft bread, hunks of cheese, and apples had been realistically provided in our haversacks.

These, rashly crammed into our mouths, made our enunciation almost unintelligible. However, we hastily finished our lines (and our food) and progressed gingerly towards the doors at the back of the stalls, only to find them locked impenetrably against our exit. So we had to walk back along the ramp the way we had come, and sneak as unobtrusively as we could round the characters on the stage who were already engaged in playing another scene.

After the episode in which Joseph and Mary arrived at the inn and were given shelter in the stable, there was supposed to be a blackout, during which the Child was born, to be discovered later in the manger with the Virgin and the animals. But the light cues were fatally mismanaged, and the gauze, supposed to conceal the stable during an interlude played in front of it, suddenly became transparent. Fay Compton could be plainly seen picking up the doll representing the infant Jesus by its heels out of the crib and swathing it with a napkin before setting it on her lap. Ellen Terry, who had been brought by her daughter to make an appeal at the beginning of the performance, and was now sitting in the prompt corner, eagerly listening to all that was going on, peered through her thick spectacles at Fay Compton and called out in her famous Terry whisper, 'Do tell that child to take all that red off her lips.'

Ted Craig was a great disappointment to me when I met him first. C. B. Cochran had invited him to England to design an opening production for the Phoenix Theatre, which had just been completed in 1930. Sidney Bernstein had built it and had engaged Komisarjevsky to decorate it. Sidney lent Craig his London house to stay in and he was given *carte blanche* by Cochran to decide on the play he would choose to design and perhaps also to direct. I was acting at the Old Vic at the time, my second season there, and *The Tempest*, in which I was playing Prospero, had just been added to the repertoire. Of course I was greatly excited at the prospect of meeting my famous second cousin. As a schoolboy I had devoured his books, the more enthusiastically since Ellen Terry herself had given me one of them, *On the Art of the Theatre*, as a Christmas present with a dedication written on the title page. Craig invited me to lunch at the Café Royal. With him was Martin

Shaw, a clever musician and one of Craig's oldest and dearest friends. They had produced *Dido and Aeneas* and *Acis and Galatea* together in Hampstead at the beginning of the century. Martin Shaw was disfigured by a large birthmark on one side of his face, and, according to one account, Edy had once been in love with him, but Ellen had considered him too ill-looking for her daughter.

Craig treated me somewhat patronisingly at this first meeting. He said, 'I felt we ought to get to know each other, as you seem to be quite popular here in London.' He went on to say that he had rushed from the Old Vic in horror after seeing only the opening scene of *The Tempest*, though Harcourt Williams, who had directed the production, was one of his old friends and fellow actors. Ted had written to him several times during our rehearsals, wishing him luck and predicting success for him, and Harcourt Williams had continually held him up to us all as a great man and an acknowledged genius of the theatre, so I was naturally very hurt by his airy dismissal of Lilian Baylis, the Vic, and all it stood for. Naturally, too, my vanity was piqued that he had seen so little of my own performance. I asked him shyly what play he was proposing to do for Cochran. 'Oh,' he answered vaguely, 'I am not sure yet. Perhaps *Macbeth*. I have many schemes and designs for that play. But, you know, what I do look forward to is inviting any artists or friends who may be in London at the time to sit with me in the Royal Box and watch rehearsals.' I took this remark with a grain of salt, but throughout our meal I felt that he was probably posing a good deal and pulling my leg. Still, I went away with a great sense of disappointment. Not long afterwards the whole project with Cochran ended in smoke and Craig went back to Italy, and it was many years – twenty-two to be exact – before I was to see him again.

In 1953 I had rented a villa in the South of France for a summer holiday, and decided to look him up in Vence, where he was living on little money at a small pension. My sister and I drove up a steep lane to find it, and there, standing at the top of a flight of stone steps, was Craig – unmistakably impressive in a broadbrimmed straw hat, with a walking stick (probably Irving's) in his hand, large tortoiseshell spectacles on his nose, a scarf thrown round his neck, and a frieze Italian

cloak flung back over a white coat like a surgeon's, with a
high collar, and some kind of medallion on a black cord round
his neck. He looked very like the famous Toulouse-Lautrec
poster of Aristide Bruant. He seemed enormously pleased to
welcome us, sang snatches of music-hall songs, cracked jokes,
and told us the best restaurant to eat at. Of course we took
him there immediately and helped him to enjoy a delicious
meal. Then he took us back to the pension and showed us
his small room, touchingly simple and beautifully arranged.
Small photographs were pinned on a screen and above his
narrow little bed with its folded rug. Pipes, drawing instruments, knives and chisels, all impeccably tidy, were laid out
in order on his desk. He had created a little world of his own
in those modest surroundings. On a shelf were copies of
mid-Victorian farces which he had collected on the quais in
Paris and bound and annotated himself. Books were piled
everywhere but he seemed to know exactly where to find any
reference he wanted. He seemed contented and delightfully
affable, and when he came to see us at our villa a few days
later he charmed us as greatly as before. I noticed that he
never spoke French – even in the restaurant, where the pro-
prietress and waiters knew him well – and he seemed amazingly well informed about the theatre in London and indeed
everywhere in Europe. He had met Laurence Olivier in Paris,
where he had seen him play Richard the Third, and thought
his performance fine and Irvingesque. I told him I had heard
he had gone to see it several times. 'Yes,' he replied, 'I am
getting deaf you know, and they used to let me pop into the
prompter's box so that I could see and hear really well.'
'Surely not *every* night,' I said. 'Well, occasionally I used to
slip out and sit for a bit of a smoke in the box-office,' he
admitted, chuckling. 'And do you know, about nine o'clock
every evening a man would come in and take a big bag of
money away with him. Of course that impressed me very
much!'

We had broken the ice at last on these two visits, and I was
deeply touched when, at a time of great trouble for me in
London a few months later he suddenly wrote me a letter
enclosing a card in Ellen Terry's handwriting, which she had
sent to comfort him on some occasion, years before, when
he had been involved in a disturbing crisis of his own.

After that time we wrote to each other fairly often, and I went to see him again whenever I was in the South of France. After long negotiations he had managed to sell his fine library to a French collector, and with the money had bought a small bungalow on the outskirts of Vence, where he was looked after by his daughter Nellie, a charming middle-aged woman, about my sister's age, with a great look of her grandmother and a gentle voice. He was ninety now, deaf, toothless, and very frail, but still full of energy and fun. He was lying on his bed when we arrived to take him out to lunch, reading a little book of Elizabethan poems. I asked Nellie to come with us (at which she seemed rather surprised, as she had expected to be left at home) and we got into the car with Ted in front. He chose a restaurant some fifteen miles away and seemed delighted at the prospect of quite a long drive. 'Don't talk at the back there,' he shouted to us, 'I can't hear a word you're saying.' Then he handed the book of poems to me across the back of his seat. 'Read this one,' he said, 'it's supposed to be by Walter Raleigh, but it's far too good for that. I bet it's Shakespeare. You ought to read it in your Recital, John, I hear you're having a great success with your readings.' 'All right,' I said, 'if you'll copy it out in your beautiful hand-writing and send it to me.' But, alas he never did.

We chattered and laughed together over an enormous lunch, and it was after four o'clock when we got back to his little villa. When I said goodbye he put his hands on my shoulders and kissed me sweetly on both cheeks, and I felt sure I would not see him again.

Was Craig a genius? Thinking of him the other day I suddenly wondered why on earth I did not ask him to design *Macbeth* for me when I directed and played in it in 1942 – but then of course the War was raging, and he could not easily have come to England. (He was actually interned in Paris by the Nazis, but released after a few months with the help of Sylvia Beach, the publisher, and some Germans who had always admired his work.) But I fancy he would always have proved very difficult to handle if he had ever got down to the concrete task of producing a play. He was didactic and uncompromising, but also frivolous and unpredictable, as one can easily see from his son Edward's superb biography. Apart from the management who engaged him would he have known how to deal with actors and actresses? Would he have been patient and tactful enough to direct them, as he always seemed to expect to be allowed to do, as well as collaborating successfully with the technicians in creating the décor and lighting? He suffered from persecution mania, relying on other people yet trusting hardly anyone. He could not bring himself to confide in those who tried or offered to carry out his ideas for fear they would steal or misinterpret them. Autocratic to a degree, wildly egotistical, fickle and utterly unprincipled where money and women were concerned, he still created for himself a mystique of enduring proportions. A master without a school, an Englishman hardly acknowledged in his own country, he influenced the whole development of the theatre both in Europe and America. He abolished footlights and experimented with the spatial limits of the stage both in his designs and in one or two of the few productions which he actually achieved, framing his scenes in higher and wider proscenium openings and creating effects of simplicity and grandeur. He used a cyclorama for the first time, and the movable screens which he designed for the Moscow Arts production of *Hamlet* by Stanislavsky (though they failed to be completely successful on that occasion through lack of technical equipment to manipulate them), were a really magnificent invention. His passion for research was indefatigable. He was a voracious reader and an untiring worker. Very beautiful as a young man, his features still had a certain weakness which remained even when he was very old. Temperamental, crackety, with a charming voice and aristocratic manner, he was an artist to his finger tips. His thumbs however were rather sinister – unnaturally broad and thick. Quarrelsome and tender, violent one minute and gentle the next, he must always have been what nurses used to call 'a handful'!

26

THREE WITTY LADIES

MRS PATRICK CAMPBELL, LADY TREE, AND DAME LILIAN BRAITHWAITE

MRS PATRICK CAMPBELL

'Stella – Stella for Star,' cried the heroine of Tennessee Williams's *Streetcar Named Desire*. And I thought at once of another star – Stella Beatrice, the great actress Mrs Patrick Campbell. Brilliant, impossible, cruel, fascinatingly self-destructive, witty (especially when she had a foeman worthy of her steel – Herbert Tree, Bernard Shaw, or Noël Coward), devastatingly unpredictable, she could be grandly snobbish one minute and generously simple the next. She despised people who were afraid of her, would patronise an audience if she felt them to be unsympathetic, and make fun of her fellow actors if they failed to provide her with inspiration. I once saw her walk through the whole of the first act of *John Gabriel Borkman*, ignoring the other players and taking every other line from the prompter, only to electrify the house in the next scene when she was partnered by an actor she admired. Her stage movements were expressive and unlike those of any other actress. I can see her now in *The Second Mrs Tanqueray* (late in her career, on tour at a theatre in Croydon), peeling muscat grapes with her fingers and cramming them into her mouth, 'I adore fruit, especially when it's expensive'; stabbing the hat on her lap with a furious hatpin as Mrs Cortelyon left the stage in the second act, and gazing at her face in a hand-mirror at the end of the play just before her final exit. I see her opening champagne in *Ghosts*, laying a table, cooing to a baby, and digging into a hamper of old clothes in *The Matriarch*, knitting in the last act of *Pygmalion* with a look of unutterable boredom on her face, airing her newly taught society accent in hollow, supercilious tones.

She was beginning to be fat when I met her first, and would make constant references to her fast-vanishing figure. 'I look like a burst paper bag,' and, 'I must borrow a chair with a high back so that I can hide my chins behind it.' She nearly always wore sweeping black dresses and hats with shady brims (she once told me proudly that the hat she was wearing that day looked so much better since she had trimmed the edges of it with a pair of nail-scissors), and her flowing velvets were usually sprinkled with the white hairs of Moonbeam, her beloved Pekinese. But she still appeared majestic as she swept down in the hotel lift to enthrone herself in a New York taxi, where she would proceed to chat with the driver on a variety of topics – the stupidity of Hollywood, the Abdication of the Duke of Windsor ('Such a gesture has not been made since Antony gave up a Kingdom for Cleopatra') or the necessity of a halt to walk her dog. 'Who's responsible for this?' the man demanded as he discovered a puddle on the floor of his cab. 'I am,' replied Mrs Campbell, as she alighted calmly.

Everyone referred to her as Mrs Pat, but I always hated the familiarity, and took care always to address her by her full name until the day when she rewarded me by asking me to call her Stella. I had been introduced to her, in the early Twenties, at a luncheon party in Brighton in a private suite at the Metropole Hotel given by a Lord who loved the stage. She was playing Hedda Gabler at a theatre on one of the piers (why didn't I go to see her in it?) and someone told her that the performance was a *tour de force*. 'I suppose that is why I am always forced to tour,' she replied mournfully. Her company dreaded her, except for the few worshippers who dared to stand up to her when she was in a bad mood. She loved rich and titled people and would allow them to give her presents and entertain her, but she was very proud with younger folk and generous both in advice and criticism. She could be wonderful company, though I think she was often cruel to men who fell in love with her – even Forbes-Robertson and Shaw – and sometimes even more unkind to her women friends, letting them fetch and carry for her for a time and then making fun of them or casting them aside. But somehow I was never afraid of her, though the only time I acted with her, as Oswald in *Ghosts* in 1929, she played some alarming tricks and made a fool of me at one performance. The dress-rehearsal had gone off without mishap, and Mrs Campbell was word perfect and sailing through her scenes. At the first performance, however, she seemed less at ease, though still charming to me at the fall of the curtain, when she graciously thanked me for having helped her through. I beamed with delight and thought I had passed my test. At the second performance I was sitting at a table smoking. No ash tray had been provided, and I looked helplessly round when the cue came for me to put out my cigar. Not daring to leave my chair, for fear of complicating the moves that had been arranged by the director, I stubbed it out on the chenille tablecloth and dropped the butt under the table and then, a few moments later, stupidly put my hands on the table before lifting them to cover my face. Mrs Campbell, turning upstage, shook with laughter for the rest of the scene, and pouted, 'Oh, you're such an amateur!' as the curtain fell. During the second interval my aunt, Mabel Terry-Lewis, never famous for her tact, burst into my dressing-room. 'Tell her we can't hear a word she says,' she announced, 'the Charing Cross Road is being drilled outside!' This counsel I naturally preferred to ignore, though it hardly tended to improve my already shaken confidence. But worse was yet to come. At the end of the play Mrs Alving stands aghast, staring at her son as he mutters, 'Mother, give me the sun. The sun! The sun!' In her hand she still holds the box of pills which she does not dare to give him. Mrs Campbell had evidently decided suddenly that she must make the most of this important final moment. With a wild cry, she flung the pillbox into the footlights and threw herself across my knees with her entire weight. 'Oswald. Oswald!' she moaned. The armchair (borrowed by Mrs Campbell herself from a friend, because, as she said, 'the back is high enough to hide my chins') cracked ominously as she lay prone across my lap, and as I clutched the arms in desperation for fear they might disintegrate, she whispered fiercely, 'Keep down for the call. This play is worse than having a confinement.' Yet she had been of the greatest help during rehearsals and I always thought she could, if she had chosen, have been a fine director herself.

It was very difficult to judge the extent of her real talents in those later days. Of course I never saw her at the time of her early triumphs, when she was slim and elegant and Aubrey Beardsley drew her, willow-slender, for an exquisite study in black-and-white. I think she never took much exercise – the leading ladies of her day didn't deign to walk – and she was very fond of food. During the rehearsals of *Ghosts* we would lunch together, and she would sit in the Escargot Restaurant, devouring snails by the dozen. One day, while we were there, a striking-looking lady, with black hair parted in the middle and drawn back in a great knot at the nape of her neck, appeared in the doorway, attracting considerable attention from everyone in the room. 'Surely that is Madame Marguerite D'Alvarez, the famous singer,' I ventured to remark. Mrs Campbell lifted her eyes from her plate and murmured in tragic tones, 'Ah yes, Me in a spoon.'

I thought she did not much care for the Terry family, for my great-aunt Marion had been a famous rival of hers. She had played Mrs Erlynne on one occasion in Dublin to Mrs Campbell's Lady Windermere, and taken over her part at the last moment when Mrs Campbell quarrelled with Forbes-Robertson during the rehearsals of Henry Arthur Jones' *Michael and his Lost Angel*, though Marion proved to be ill-suited and the play was a complete failure. They were to play together once more in the 1920 revival of *Pygmalion*, and I fancy that she and Mrs Campbell must have worked on this occasion with velvet gloves. But she always spoke to me of Ellen Terry with great admiration though she could not resist one crushing remark about my mother's family. I had been distressed to find her in New York (this was in 1936), living without a maid in a second-rate hotel room, clothes and papers strewn everywhere, laid up with influenza. She wrote afterwards to Shaw that my eyes had filled with tears when I arrived. 'All the Terrys cry so easily,' was her typical comment. But when I tried to send her a cheque as a Christmas present she refused to accept it and sent it back.

One afternoon, while I was playing *Hamlet* in New York,

Mrs Campbell offered to take me to visit Edward Sheldon, the playwright. This remarkable man had been a youthful friend of John Barrymore, and had encouraged him to further his stage career by the brilliant series of classical revivals and romantic plays (*Richard III, Hamlet,* Tolstoy's *Living Corpse, The Jest*) in which Barrymore triumphed in the early Twenties. Sheldon was also the author of two sensationally successful melodramas, *Salvation Nell* for Mrs Fiske and *Romance* for Doris Keane, with whom he had been very much in love. He was now completely paralysed and blind as a result of some petrifying bone disease, but, despite his infirmity, he retained all his intellectual faculties, and continued his friendship with all the most brilliant players of the New York theatre, who went continually to see him and greatly valued his advice.

I realised, of course, that it was a great compliment to be given the opportunity of this meeting, and arrived punctually at the address in the East Sixties where he lived. Mrs Campbell was not yet there, and I was somewhat dismayed to be shown up to the penthouse, where I was ushered into a big lofty room with many windows looking out on to a terrace. Flowers, photographs, and books were everywhere, and there was no feeling of a sickroom except for the great bed, covered with a dark brocade coverlet, on which Sheldon lay stretched out, and his head tilted back at what seemed a dreadfully low and uncomfortable angle. His smooth face was beautifully shaved and he wore a neat bow tie and a soft shirt, but his eyes were covered with a black mask, and his hands were invisible beneath the coverlet.

Of course I was very shy at first, but as soon as he began to talk (though with a grating tired voice) he managed immediately to put me at my ease, and by the time Mrs Campbell arrived we were chattering away as if we had known each other all our lives.

Books and newspapers were read to him every day, and he was amazingly well-informed, especially about the theatre, and seemed to know everything that was going on. He asked me if I would come again one day and act some scenes from *Hamlet* for him, and of course I promised to do so. Again, he contrived to put me at my ease, and I never played to a more sensitive and appreciative audience.

In the years that followed he never forgot me, sending cables and messages even during the war years (he was destined to live longer than Mrs Campbell, who died in 1940) and when I was acting in Congreve's *Love for Love* in 1944 I received a telegram 'How I wish I could see you in Valentine's mad scene.'[1]

On that first afternoon, Mrs Campbell appeared ten minutes after I did. I fancy Sheldon had asked her to be late, so that he could break the ice with me alone. She was in one of her complaining moods, pouting and holding up her Pekinese against Sheldon's face, sighing that nobody wanted her any more in the theatre now that she was old and fat. Sheldon suddenly grew very quiet, and I noted how quickly she changed her manner and began to behave and talk in the fascinating, brilliant way that showed her at her very best. When we went away I tried to tell her how much I appreciated her charming gesture in taking me to see Sheldon and how delightfully she had helped to entertain us both. 'Ah,' she said, with real sincerity, 'one has to be at one's best with Ned. After all, we are all he has left. Think of it. There he lies in that room up there which he will never leave, and here we are walking in the street in the sunshine.' I never loved her more than on that day.

In a lecture recital which she concocted in the early Thirties, I realised that she was a complete Pre-Raphaelite. Neither Shakespeare nor the Bible served to exhibit her to real advantage. She boomed too much, sometimes even verging upon absurdity. I once saw her attempt Lady Macbeth, appearing with the American actor James Hackett, and she evidently did not care for acting with him. She had one fine moment at the end of the banquet scene, when she wearily dragged the crown from her head and her black hair fell to her shoulders as she sat huddled on the throne. But on her first appearance, looking like the Queen of Hearts about to have the gardeners executed, she swept her eyes over the stalls, graciously bowed to acknowledge her reception – leading ladies always entered to applause in those days – and, solemnly unrolling a large scroll (which, as one critic remarked, it would have taken a whole monastery a month to illuminate!), she read out Macbeth's letter with stately emphasis but ill-concealed contempt. In her

[1] The remarkable memories of the older well-educated generation are very striking. Mr Justice Frankfurter, a famous American High Court Judge, quoted verbatim the whole opening scene of *Love for Love* when I met him in Washington at supper after the performance.

recital, however, the excerpts from Pinero, Shaw, and Ibsen were very fine, and I was especially impressed by her rendering of *The High Tide on the Lincolnshire Coast*, a Victorian poem by Jean Ingelow. Her success with this made me realise why she had been so greatly in demand at parties in the Nineties, when she would recite (no doubt for an enormous fee) 'Butterflies all White – Butterflies all Black', in competition with Sarah Bernhardt, who was also a fashionable diseuse at the smart houses in those days whenever she acted in London. The two stars became great cronies, and on one occasion they played *Pelléas and Mélisande* together in French. Mrs Campbell had played Mélisande before with Martin Harvey and Forbes-Robertson, and in her recital she used to give an excerpt from the play (in English naturally), delivering the speeches of both the lovers in two contrasting voices, but this was not a very happy experiment as it seemed to me. The two actresses were fond of exchanging long telegrams with one another. I think Stella was not, as Ellen Terry was, an inspired letter-writer, and her correspondence with Shaw compares very poorly with that of Ellen. But I well remember a small luncheon party which I gave in New York when Mrs Campbell read to us aloud an article she had written on Bernhardt for a theatre magazine. This was charmingly written and immensely moving, and of course drew more 'Terry tears' from me.

She had always been amused to shock people by her behaviour, though she was sometimes rather prudish too, and I took care never to make ambiguous jokes when I was with her. My mother told me that once at a dinner party, when Stella was first married, she made a sensation, as the ladies rose to leave the table, by seizing a handful of cigars as they were being passed to the gentlemen by a servant, and, sticking them boldly in her *décolletage* one by one, announced gaily, 'Poor Pat can't afford cigars.'

Her witticisms have become a legend. Of Noël Coward's dialogue, 'His characters talk like typewriting.' Of a leading lady she was acting with, 'Her eyes are so far apart that you want to take a taxi from one to the other.' 'Tell Mr Alexander (who was playing Tanqueray) I never laugh at him while we are on the stage together. I always wait till I get home.' Of Shaw, 'One day he will eat a beefsteak, and then God help us poor women.' But Alexander Woollcott's famous remark after

her Hollywood film débâcle a few years before she died, 'She
is like a sinking ship firing on its rescuers,' was sadly to the
point. She became impossibly difficult, insulted managers who
made her offers, appeared in one or two absurdly bad plays,
and made them worse by clowning in the serious scenes and
assuming a tragic manner in the light ones. When she was appearing in a light comedy of Ivor Novello's in New York, for
instance, she insisted on interpolating a speech from *Electra* in
the middle of a most unsuitable context. But she never lost her
sense of style or her regal bearing, and the deep voice, so often
imitated, retained its thrilling range and power. James Agate
still talked of 'the questing sweep of her throat' and her feet and
ankles were slim and elegant to the last.

I read one of the lessons at her Memorial Service in 1941, on
the morning following a first night at the Old Vic at which I
had essayed King Lear. Coming out of the Church I heard
someone say, 'It was an exciting occasion at the Old Vic last
night,' and the answer, 'Yes, until the curtain went up,' was, I
felt, one that Stella's shade would have surely relished. She
might so easily have delivered it herself.

Review of Mrs Pat *biography by Margot Peters*

Published by the Bodley Head

When I first met Mrs Patrick Campbell in the Twenties, at a
lunch party at the Metropole Hotel in Brighton, her days of
great success were long over. I had heard, of course, many of
the legendary tales about her, but I stupidly failed to realise that
by this time she was beset by chronic financial difficulties and
personal squabbles, and was forced to tour, playing on seaside
piers · and anywhere else in the provinces and outskirts of
London in which she could manage to obtain an engagement,
at a poor salary, in her once-famous roles Paula Tanqueray,
Hedda Gabler. She was now too old and fat for these, though
still able, when she chose, to act with something of her former
fire and power.

The paradoxical glamour of her personality and her defiant
humour fascinated me immediately, and I was greatly flattered
when she seemed to take a fancy to me and to express an
interest in my own ambitious career.

I had found her autobiography, when it was first published in 1922, sadly disappointing, full of gushing tributes from titled admirers, poets and painters, but failing to convey anything of her own unique distinction. Alan Dent's account of her, written in 1961, was, to me, equally unsatisfactory. He had, I believe, never seen her act, and relied largely on the memories of James Agate (to whom Dent was secretary), who admired her very much. The result was untidy and only sporadically interesting.

I myself only saw her on the stage about half-a-dozen times, and acted with her only once (Agate described her Mrs Alving as being 'like the Lord Mayor's Coach with nothing in it'). I even attempted to direct her on one occasion, in a play which she sadly abandoned after a few weeks' rehearsal. But the brilliant biography by Mrs Peters has been researched with exemplary care and accuracy. The famous *bons mots* nearly always witty, sometimes cruel and personal, but usually devastatingly apt are quoted with appropriate relish. There is a wealth of material, never before made public, to enthrall the reader: the love affair with Forbes-Robertson (unfortunately no letters exist between them); the two broken marriages to Patrick Campbell and George Cornwallis-West; the fantastic popular acclaim, in both England and America, in the first years of this century, following the sensational Nineties' success of Mrs Tanqueray; the slogging tours and special matinées; the money squandered, generously as well as self-indulgently.

Then comes the slow but inevitable decline, largely, alas, of her own making. She became, as the American critic Alexander Woollcott remarked, 'a sinking ship, firing on her rescuers'. She could not cure herself of her deliberately contemptuous attitude towards her audiences as well as to managers and fellow-players. In her private life came the tragic wartime death of her beloved spoilt son and quarrels with his widow and her long-suffering daughter. Her acting career was to end with the wretched fiasco of her experiences in Hollywood. Her final days of exile and illness are infinitely sad.

Best of all, perhaps, are the chapters dealing with the abortive love affair with Shaw, who carefully guarded her infatuated letters until his wife's death, and which Mrs

Campbell bargained so desperately to sell for publication in their last years. His baffling experiences with her in *Pygmalion*, and subsequent refusal to allow her, in several of his later plays, to create the parts which she herself had inspired (Hesione in *Heartbreak House*, the Serpent in *Back to Methuselah*), her pleas for money, and their mutual disillusionment – all this makes fascinating reading. Amidst such wealth of detail, there is a sentence which one would be glad to have elucidated even further. 'Duse had played Mrs Tanqueray's suicide – in front of the audience – and still felt it would be worthless to play it in any other way!' Could Duse have actually produced a phial and expired in a scene which Pinero never wrote? The opportunity offered of such a striking solo curtain would no doubt have appealed to Mrs Campbell. She obviously resented (when I acted with her in Ibsen's *Ghosts*) that Oswald has the final words.

Mrs Peters perceptively sums up Mrs Campbell's whole life and career when she writes:

A strong sense of the absurd saved her from taking it all too seriously. 'My eyes are nothing in particular,' she would remark of her most admired feature. 'God gave me boot-buttons, but I invented the dreamy eyelid and that makes all the difference.'

LADY TREE

Lady Tree, *née* Maud Holt, had been a medical student and a Greek scholar before she became a successful actress. In her early photographs she appears pretty and slight, but when I first saw her on the stage, and later when I came to meet her, she had become somewhat eccentric-looking, wearing strikingly coloured flowing robes and fantastic hats, with scarves and veils draped about her throat and shoulders. She was supposed to have been a most moving Ophelia, when her husband, Sir Herbert Beerbohm Tree, played Hamlet. In his fair wig and beard Max Beerbohm is said to have remarked that he looked like a German Professor, and described his performance as being 'funny without being vulgar', though

Max was always too much of a gentleman to attack his half-brother in his official notices in the *Saturday Review*.

Invited to see a play one evening by some enthusiastic friends, Max was somewhat dismayed to be ushered into a box at His Majesty's to see a performance of *Hamlet*. During the evening his hosts looked round to find his chair unoccupied, but soon found him curled up on a pile of overcoats in the passage, dozing. He woke and murmured apologetically, 'I am so sorry. I always enjoy Herbert's Hamlet this way.'

Sir Herbert was brilliant and eccentric too. He emulated a number of his contemporaries in siring several offspring besides those already presented him by his wife. Lady Tree, playing hostess, was once heard to remark, 'Ah, Herbert, late again? Another confinement in Putney?' And one night, returning late from a party to find Sir Herbert supping *tête à tête* with Esmé Percy, an extremely handsome young actor in his company, she peeped in at the door and murmured, 'The port's on the sideboard, Herbert, and remember it's adultery just the same.'

Many years later she was acting in *The Mask of Virtue*, a comedy in an eighteenth-century setting adapted from the French, in which Vivien Leigh made her first success in London. At the dress rehearsal Lady Tree, gazing hopefully across the empty stalls, called to the director, 'Mr A., it seems a little dark on the stage in this scene. Could you oblige us with a little more light? I think you may not have realised that my comedic effects in this play are almost wholly grimacial.'

At a charity matinée in which I once appeared with her she surveyed her script at rehearsals through an enormous magnifying glass. I was told that she would bring *The Times* Crossword Puzzle into the wings with her and proceed to solve it during her waits, uttering strange syllabic gasps and grunts to find the word of the exact length and shape she needed. Once in a modern comedy, *Indoor Fireworks*, she seemed to have threaded a lace scarf from one side of her head to the other, passing it through her large red wig and finally tying it under her chin like a bonnet, achieving a very strange result. One day I was lunching in a Soho restaurant, before playing a matinée, and saw her arrive at a neighbouring table with her daughter Viola. Not expecting her to remember me I bowed respectfully in passing them as I rose to go. Halfway down the street I heard my name called after me in dulcet tones, and, looking back, saw Lady Tree standing in the doorway of the restaurant, waving her scarf at me in belated greeting like Isolde or some Arthurian heroine of romance.

When she lay dying in hospital, her lawyer came to see her to help her to put her affairs in order. When he had gone away, her daughter asked her if his visit had not too greatly tired her. 'Not at all,' said Lady Tree, 'he was just teaching me my death duties.'

DAME LILIAN BRAITHWAITE

I knew Dame Lilian Braithwaite very well, and also had the delight of working with her very often. Since her early days as a successful *ingénue*, she had acted in every kind of play – farce, melodrama, Shakespeare – and was already a well-known leading lady in a number of West End plays at the time of the First World War. She was considered at that time to be a somewhat sentimental actress of sympathetic parts. But when she made an astonishing success as the vapid manhunting society mother in Noël Coward's *The Vortex* in 1924, critics and public were full of praise for her courage in daring to play with such honesty and conviction. From this new success she continued from one triumph to another both in light comedies and dramatic plays. Her witty timing, which she used to perfection both on and off the stage, gave a delicious edge to what seemed at first a deceptively innocent air of conventional Edwardian charm. Her kindness was unfailing, but the subtlety of the pause she would give to cap a critical remark could be delightfully pungent and occasionally devastating. 'B. told me that she is off to do a play in New York tomorrow . . . but I don't think it can be a very big part as she is going on a very small boat.' 'Of course I'm very fond of G. . . . , but I know what people mean.' I was with her once at a matinée. One of the leading actresses appearing in the play was known to be distinctly plain, but in a romantic-looking photograph displayed in the programme she appeared as a raving beauty. Lilian glanced at the picture, murmured, 'Fancy!' and quickly turned the page. She was a beautiful woman, always looking cool and elegant both on and off the stage, and she managed her cooing voice and precise diction with impeccable skill. She could drawl in an affected part or dominate in a dramatic scene with unexpected power. I used to watch her, fascinated, as she waited to make her first entrance in *The Vortex*, standing behind the closed door at which she was to appear, bracing herself with deep breaths, like an athlete preparing for a race, before she opened it.

She was a worthy opponent for some of her witty contemporaries, and could even challenge Mrs Campbell and Marie Tempest on their own ground, if either of them tried to patronise her, as they sometimes did. Lunching at the Ivy Restaurant one day with her daughter, a very unattractive man appeared in the doorway. The *maître d'hôtel* enquired politely, 'You want a table, sir? For two?' 'No,' replied the man, 'I'm quite alone.' Lilian was heard to mutter, 'I'm not surprised.'

Her enthusiasm and gallantry never failed her. In the Second War she went on organising concerts and entertainments for ENSA as well as appearing herself with unfailing professionalism and punctuality in the theatre in several long and arduous runs. Returning late one night after acting in *Arsenic and Old Lace*, she took refuge in the ground floor cloakroom during a big air-raid lasting for many hours. Asked the next morning if she was not exhausted by the experience she replied smilingly, 'Certainly not. We were fifty pounds up last night.' To a young actress who rashly remarked, 'Oh, I am so sorry you were in front this afternoon. I always feel I must save myself for the evening performance,' Lilian only shook her head, 'I didn't think you saved anything,' she said. And at a magnificent party to celebrate a long run she pointed to her dress with the remark 'C. has given me a dear little diamond brooch . . . can you see it?'

Actresses seemed in my youth to achieve astonishing changes in their figures in order to suit the fashions of the time. Lilian Braithwaite, a wasp-waisted slim *ingénue* in her early photographs, looked almost ample when I first saw her, during the First War, as the heroine's mother in a play at the Haymarket, *General Post*, with Norman McKinnel, Madge Titheradge, and George Tully. But ten years later she was as slim as a reed in the tubular frocks, short skirts, and shingled hair of the dancing mother in *The Vortex*. Even Ellen Terry, graceful and elegant until the end of the last century, appears matronly and almost stout in the photographs of her in *Captain Brassbound's Conversion* in 1906, though she too became extremely slender in her old age. Yet these were the days before dieting and beauty parlours. Marie Tempest was always plump and Yvonne Arnaud increasingly so as time went on. Lilian could not resist saying of her, 'It's still the dear little face we all loved so in *By Candle Light* (Pause) – but there's another face round it.'

The three actresses in this chapter might have perhaps been ideally cast as the three Queens in *Alice in Wonderland* – their dialogue precisely to the point, their wit as characteristically individual as their delightful and original personalities. Their witticisms would certainly have provided remarkable copy for anyone lucky enough to overhear what they had to say to one another behind the scenes.

27

SOME NON-ACTING ACTORS

SIR CHARLES HAWTREY, ALLAN AYNESWORTH, GERALD DU MAURIER, RONALD SQUIRE, A. E. MATTHEWS

Smart drawing-room comedy has always been staple fare in the London theatre, and Max Beerbohm, in one of his theatre notices of the early 1900s, writes mockingly of the absurdly over-tailored 'mimes' (as he always called the actors) with their impeccable trouserings with knife-edged creases and their over-polished hats and boots. But there were a number of fine players of that generation who could carry off their contemporary clothes with a more natural air.

Gerald du Maurier, for instance, used to wear old suits on the stage that were beautifully cut, but had obviously hung in his wardrobe for years. How fascinating he was, to men as well as women, although he was not at all conventionally handsome. He could slouch and lounge and flick his leading lady behind one ear as he played a love-scene, never seeming to raise his voice or force an emotion, yet he could be infinitely touching too without being in the least sentimental. His drunken painter, Dearth, in *Dear Brutus*, was a masterpiece of understatement, acted with a mixture of infinite charm and regretful pathos. He could be flippant in light comedy or casually efficient in plays like *Raffles* and *Bulldog Drummond*. His technique was inimitably resourceful, though so well concealed. In one of his late successes, *Interference*, he held the audience enthralled while he examined a murdered man's body in a long scene lasting several silent minutes, and once, when he played a walk-on valet at a charity matinée he managed to make an effective moment as he took the overcoat from the shoulders of one of the principal characters.

Charles Hawtrey and Allan Aynesworth belonged to the same naturalistic school as du Maurier, and, after their deaths Ronald Squire and A. E. Matthews continued the same kind of tradition on similar lines though they never achieved quite so much success.

Hawtrey and Aynesworth were both portly and well fed, looking more like business men than actors. They wore dark suits for formal occasions, their tweeds or riding breeches for the country were unobtrusively well cut, and their coats were roomy with big flapped pockets. They wore fancy waistcoats, gold watch-chains, and smart boots, and everything they did on the stage was perfect, so perfect that they did not seem to be acting at all. But of course they never experimented far from their own brilliant but limited range. One could never imagine them playing in Ibsen, Chekhov, Shakespeare, Sheridan, or Congreve. They might simply have strolled in for an hour or two for a little exercise as a change from sitting in their clubs. In a period when other actors took hours making-up their faces, whether as juveniles or heavily disguised character-men, their faces looked more natural than anyone else's on the stage. And yet I believe they might have been equally distinguished if they had ventured into more ambitious fields.

At the end of his career, when he was past eighty, Aynesworth played Lord Conyngham in the opening scene of Laurence Housman's *Victoria Regina*, and, partnered by my aunt, Mabel Terry-Lewis, whose distinction of bearing and diction were equal to his own, acted with a period style that put the rest of the cast to shame. And I remember meeting him once on the stone stairs at the back of the Coliseum where there was a gala matinée of *Drake*, dressed improbably as the Archbishop of Canterbury. In his robes and mitre, he looked magnificently authentic and not in the least ridiculous. But his dignified, witty approach to contemporary characters fitted his manner and personality to perfection and there were always new light comedies, however trivial, with parts in them to suit him. He was as solemnly humorous as the butler

in Milne's *The Dover Road*, one thumb tucked slyly into a
waistcoat pocket, as in playing the lovable monster Lord
Porteous in Maugham's *The Circle*, fulminating as he lost his
temper and his false teeth over the bridge table. How delightful he must have been when he created Algy in *The Importance
of Being Earnest*. He had just the right kind of urbane flippancy,
so hard to achieve for the young actors of today, especially
in the second act – the Piccadilly dandy Bunburying in the
country.

Sir George Alexander, of course, created the part of John
Worthing in the original production. I have been told, however, that Wilde first intended the play for Hawtrey, and took
it round to the theatre where he was acting at the time
demanding a sum down immediately. Hawtrey, usually as
hard-up and extravagant as Wilde himself, sent round to the
box-office asking them to advance the money, but this they
refused to do, on which Wilde went off to the St James's
Theatre round the corner and sold the play to Alexander.
Hawtrey had created the part of Lord Goring in Wilde's *An
Ideal Husband* at the Haymarket some years before, and I have
always been deeply shocked to read how he and Charles
Brookfield – who played Goring's valet in the same production – had rounded up a number of the more sordid
witnesses who appeared for Queensberry in the famous libel
action. The two men gave a supper party together to celebrate
Wilde's sentence in 1895, when, of course, the enormously
successful first production of *The Importance* had to be so
suddenly taken off.

Whether Hawtrey (as well as Brookfield) had always hated
Wilde is not on record, but he would certainly have been ideal
casting for the part of Worthing. No one could tell a lie on
the stage with more superb conviction, and his scene of
mourning for his lost brother would have been the very kind
of thing he always did best. I was lucky enough to see him
in a number of plays, *The Naughty Wife* with Gladys Cooper,
a revival of Maugham's *Jack Straw*, with Lottie Venne (a
tiny, brilliant farceuse whom I also adored), and in *Ambrose
Applejohn's Adventure* by Walter Hackett, in which he was
enormously funny, wearing an eighteenth-century pirate costume (in some kind of dream or fantasy scene) and using comic
oaths, swaggering about without the slightest appearance of

Nöel Coward and Gertrude Lawrence in
Private Lives at the Pheonix Theatre,
1930

Vivien Leigh

John Barrymore as Hamlet, Theatre Royal, Haymarket, 1925

Esmé Percy

Edith Sitwell, 1928

Ernest Thesiger

Robert Farquharson in *The Cenci*
at the New Theatre, 1922

Ada King in *The Queen Was in The Parlour* at St. Martin's Theatre, 1926

Haidée Wright and Robert Loraine in *The Father* at the Everyman, Hampstead, 1927

Marie Tempest, 1906

Ronald Squire, Yvonne Arnaud and Leslie Faber in *By CandleLight* at the Prince of Wales Theatre, 1928

Hugh Sinclair and Elizabeth Bergner in *Escape Me Never*

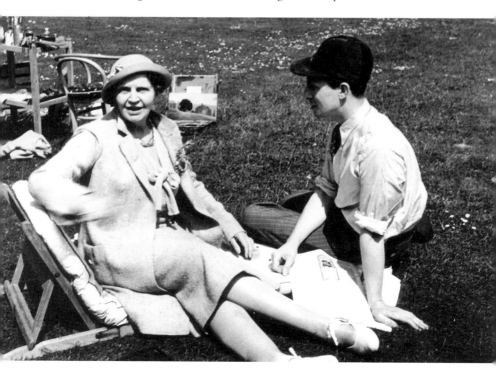

Lady Colefax and Rex Whistler at Ashcombe, c.1937

knowing how absurd he was. In Maugham's First War light comedy, *Home and Beauty*, he played the husband of the feather-headed young wife (Gladys Cooper) who, imagining him killed in battle, has rashly married again. Hawtrey entered in a clumsy reach-me-down suit which was immediately funny on his large figure, and discovering a baby in the nurse's arms, suddenly realised what had happened in his absence and brought down the curtain (and the house) with the line, 'Hell, said the Duchess!' And I can see him now trying to cook a rationed meal on the kitchen range with the help of the second husband, exquisitely polite in his exchanges with the spinsterish professional co-respondent whom he has called in to arrange a belated divorce – Jean Cadell at her most acidly respectable.

A great gambler and *bon viveur* in private life, Hawtrey achieved the same airy effect of enjoyment and leisure when he acted, passing off an embarrassing situation, eating a stage meal, or galvanising undistinguished dialogue. In his performances, as with Aynesworth's, stylishness and ease were apparent in everything he did. Entrances, exits, and stage crosses never seemed planned or theatrical, they simply seemed to happen. Diction, phrasing, and timing had been studied, practised, and then concealed, so that dialogue appeared to be completely spontaneous. Both players were solid British gentlemen, Londoners to their finger-tips. The moment they appeared on the stage one sank back comfortably in one's seat. The silk would never be creased, the wheels would revolve with infallible precision. What masters of their craft they were, and how perfectly they executed it!

Ronald Squire had often understudied Hawtrey and followed his methods to great effect. He used a very subtle throw-away technique, with his own particular distinction of personality and deadpan comedy timing. In *By Candle Light*, Lonsdale's *The Last of Mrs Cheyney*, and *On Approval*, he was the aristocratic *flâneur* or the perfect butler to his finger-tips, and in Maugham's *The Breadwinner* his rebellious stockbroker paterfamilias was equally delightful. But he also gave an unexpectedly skilful performance as the Doctor in *A Month in the Country*, with Valerie Taylor and Michael Redgrave, and would I am sure have been equally enchanting as Gaev in *The Cherry Orchard*, which he was rehearsing when the

Second War broke out and the production (by Michel St
Denis) had to be abandoned.

I once flew with him to Hollywood in 1952 when I was to
act Cassius for MGM in *Julius Caesar*, and he was to play a
supporting part in a film with Olivia de Havilland and Richard
Burton at another studio. I was much embarrassed to find
that, while he was greeted with scant ceremony, the red
carpet was rolled out for me. I was delighted, however, to
hear that, after two days' shooting, the crew working with
him had become immediately aware of his unique talents and
distinction, and treated him as an important star, though he
always loved to pretend, as did many others of the du Maurier
school, that the theatre was only a chore to be endured as a
means of making money as opposed to the more pleasurable
diversions of golf, the race course or the club.

A. E. Matthews outlived the other four players by several
years, and was still appearing, both in film studios and in the
theatre, when he was past ninety. As a young man he had
been an attractive juvenile, playing in *Peter's Mother* with
Marion Terry and in *Alice Sit By The Fire* with Ellen, and
in America he created Aynesworth's part of Algy in *The
Importance of Being Earnest*. I first saw him, during the First
War, as the leading man in the famous *Peg O' My Heart*,
Laurette Taylor's great success written by her husband J.
Hartley Manners. She herself had left the cast after a few
months, and Mary O'Farrell – afterwards famous as a radio
actress – had now taken over the part of Peg, entering with
a shaggy dog in her arms and a cardboard box for luggage.
My eldest brother was in love with her at the time and took
me in the pit one night to see the play. As Matthews entered
he whispered, 'That is the oldest juvenile in London' (a remark
which I remembered somewhat ruefully a few years ago when
I was probably the oldest Joseph Surface on record). In
later life, Matthews looked like a grumpy bloodhound, with
mulberry cheeks and pale watery eyes. He appeared, both on
and off the stage, in an amazing collection of Edwardian
clothes, jodhpurs, hacking jackets, tweed suits with check
patterns and narrow turned-up trousers, and squashed shape-
less hats.

He learned his lines very sketchily (and improvised and
gagged brilliantly when he forgot them) but he had a delight-

ful cheeky nonchalance and a solid basis of technique which
always made him a delight to watch. I directed him once in
a play and we got on together very well at the rehearsals.
Meeting him in the street some time afterwards I asked him
where he was going. 'To the Garrick Club,' he replied, and
then, quick as a flash, seeing by the look in my eye that I was
not yet a member of that august fellowship, added, 'I like the
lavatories there so much. They have handles at the sides that
help you to pull yourself up!' *The Chiltern Hundreds*, in which
he acted very late in his career was an enormous success.
Matthews dozed one night in his dressing-room and fell off
his chair on to the floor where he proceeded to continue his
nap unperturbed. The callboy, finding him there, was terrified
and rushed to the stage-manager crying, 'Mr Matthews is
dead,' but before the understudy could be sent for the actor
had woken up and strolled to his entrance as if nothing
unusual had happened. Later he summoned the boy to his
room and said to him, 'Next time you find me on the floor
I suggest you tell them, "I *think* Mr Matthews is dead."'

He created quite a furore in the press when he staged a
sit-down strike, with rugs, pillows, and a shooting-stick,
outside his house in protest against a hideous new lamp-post
that was to be erected there. The last time I saw him, at a
supper-party, he arrived late as he was still acting in the
theatre. He consumed a large supper, with a quantity of gin
and several glasses of wine, and then, apparently perfectly
sober, toddled off to appear in a location shot for a film to be
taken at some suburban tube station at two o'clock in the
morning.

Of these five comedians, Charles Hawtrey was undoubtedly the most brilliant. Both he and du Maurier were also
skilled directors, both of men and women, though I think
neither of them ever directed a classic play. But they were
the undoubted masters of a school that achieved an enormously high standard during the first twenty years of the
century, a standard founded, no doubt, on the productions
of the Kendals and the Bancrofts before both couples retired
(enormously rich and successful) in early middle age.

Hawtrey and du Maurier, despite their many years of
prosperity, spent generously and lavishly, and needed to
continue working to the end of their lives, unable to afford

to leave the stage when they began to tire. The first successes of Noël Coward, in 1924, must have shaken their confidence considerably, much in the same way as my own acting generation was shaken by the new school of Angry Young Men in 1956. Coward himself had begun his stage career with Hawtrey, and always acknowledged gratefully what he learned from him. Du Maurier trained a number of brilliant players who were to gain important positions in the theatre after his death, but he was suspicious of young highbrows, and only became fond of Coward and Charles Laughton when he met them, in his last years, and was won over by their personal charm. I think he seldom cared to see other productions than his own, and was fearful of being displaced, not realising how enormously he was respected and admired by all the young players who were beginning to be successful in the theatre.

28

TWO SPLENDID CHARACTER ACTRESSES

ADA KING AND HAIDÉE WRIGHT

Neither of these two players would have made a fortune by their looks, and neither was ever a great popular star in the commercial sense of the word, but both showed immense distinction in any part I ever saw them play.

ADA KING

Ada King had created the part of Mrs Jones, the charwoman, in Galsworthy's play, *The Silver Box*, as a member of Miss Horniman's famous company in Manchester, and among her colleagues were Basil Dean (as stage manager as well as actor), Sybil Thorndike, and Lewis Casson. When I was on tour there in the 1940s I happened to notice a delightful photograph still on display in a pub window opposite the Theatre Royal, showing the whole company grouped together, and I thought of asking if I might buy it, but of course when I was in Manchester a year or two later the pub had disappeared for ever and the photograph as well.

Ada King was short and red-faced, with sandy hair, wearing gold-rimmed pince-nez on her large turned-up nose when she was not on the stage. During the early Twenties, Basil Dean engaged her for several of his productions at the St Martin's Theatre under his ReanDean management, and it was in *RUR*, the Robot play by the Czech brothers Capek, that I saw her for the first time. She played a housekeeper, and in one scene she impressed me greatly as she rushed across the stage crying out some Biblical-sounding speech of impending doom, as Leslie Banks, terrifyingly grotesque in a kind of spaceman's uniform and helmet, climbed in through the windows at the back of the stage. I next saw her in a comic part, an old biddy sitting on the steps of her slum house, in a play by Charles McEvoy, *The Likes of 'Er*. In this play she acted with Mary Clare and the young Hermione Baddeley, who made her first big success as a violent cockney child who smashed up the stage at the climax of the play, hurling china in all directions.

Ada King was as effective in costume as in modern dress. Her performance as Roxanne's duenna in Robert Loraine's production of *Cyrano de Bergerac* (presented by Cochran and decorated by Edmund Dulac, whose fairybook illustrations had meant so much to me when I was a boy) was a delicious thumbnail sketch. Wearing a jaunty little hat with a long feather, she might have stepped straight out of an etching by Callot, while in the Thorndike–Casson *Henry the Eighth* at the Old Empire, she was pure Holbein, inimitable as the Old Lady gossiping to Anne Boleyn. Pathos and broad comedy seemed to be equally within her range, and I admired her in *The Way Things Happen* by Clemence Dane at the Ambassador's Theatre, and in Noël Coward's *The Queen Was In The Parlour* at the St Martin's, a Ruritanian melodrama in which Madge Titheradge starred with Herbert Marshall, Lady Tree, and Francis Lister. In one scene Ada King, playing the secretary of the romantic Queen, got an enormous laugh as she tiptoed back into the throne-room she had just left and murmured, 'Oh, my umbrella.'

One day I instantly recognised her as I passed her in the street. She had on her gold pince-nez, and a little furpiece was round her neck, with a sad little fox's mask clasping it together and hanging down on to her chest, like the woman in one of Katherine Mansfield's short stories. I could not resist going up to her and thanking her for the pleasure her acting had always given me, and she seemed gratified but extremely shy. Some months afterwards, when Emlyn Williams and I were going into management to act in and direct together a play he had written, we were at a loss to cast the part of an eccentric Countess, and I suddenly thought of Ada King, who had not appeared on the stage for a considerable time. We wrote to her and sent her the script, asking her to come and see us as soon as she had read it, and she arrived punctually next day at the Queen's Theatre, where we met her in the foyer. She looked much the same as ever, still the pince-nez and the fur necklet and the odd old-fashioned clothes. She sat down with us, saying she was flattered to think she should be remembered by such young men, and that she liked the part we had suggested for her. 'But,' she added firmly, 'my memory is no longer as good as it once was, and I am afraid I could not dream of accepting an engagement nowadays unless I had several weeks beforehand to study and memorise my lines.' Then she gathered up her bag and her umbrella, shook hands with us both, and stepped briskly out into Shaftesbury Avenue. It was a most touching little interview. I never saw her again.

HAIDÉE WRIGHT

Haidée Wright was also in *The Way Things Happen*, and she had, I remember, a scene with Ada King in which, like the Lion and the Unicorn, each appeared to be fighting for the crown. If Ada King emerged the winner on this occasion it may have been either because her lines were better or because she was extremely funny. Also she was more real, or seemed to be so, though she had not the sheer power of Haidée Wright's taut theatrical temperament. A tiny figure – head erect, ramrod back, and flashing eyes – one could hardly conceive of anything less funny than the acting of Haidée Wright. Like Geneviève Ward (whom I once saw in *The Aristocrat* with George Alexander), she knew how to dominate the stage with absolute authority in what my father always described as The Grand Manner.

It was to her that I wrote my first fan letter to an actress when I was still a schoolboy, after seeing her in a revival of *Milestones*. I said in the letter that I had cried my eyes out, and signed it J. Gielgud. I was somewhat saddened to receive a gracious reply addressed to Miss J. Gielgud! The play, by

Arnold Bennett and Edward Knoblock, is the drama of a
family whose various members appear in the successive episodes at three separate periods in their lives. Haidée Wright
was the spinster aunt, thwarted in early life through some
passionate romantic attachment which had gone wrong. Half-
way through the play she had a dramatic outburst, dressed in
a Victorian bonnet and a dress with a bustle, and carrying a
tiny folded parasol in the crook of her arm. In the last act she
entered leaning on a cane, and later played her final scene
crouched in a low chair before the fire, dressed in a long grey
satin gown, with a shawl over her shoulders and a lace cap
on her white hair.

She was very moving in the tiny part of the Abbess in the
Convent scene of *Cyrano* (again in the same company as Ada
King, though in this play they did not meet) and soon
afterwards I sat in the gallery to watch her first-night triumph
as Queen Elizabeth in Clemence Dane's ill-fated and unequal
play *Will Shakespeare*. Her stature might have seemed more
appropriate to Queen Victoria, but her performance immediately dismissed any such thought from one's mind. She
moved with consummate dignity and grace, wearing her fine
costumes superbly and delivering her speeches – the best in
the play – in thrilling tones. She was to play Elizabeth again
in *The Dark Lady of the Sonnets* some years later, and in Shaw's
slight but witty sketch she drew a different portrait of the
same woman, an admirable contrast of sly vanity and patriotic
fervour.

Another great performance of hers, heartbreaking in its
tragic intensity, was as the old nurse in Strindberg's *The
Father* in which she had to put her master into a straitjacket,
coaxing him with familiar words as if he were still a child.

She could make an enormous effect with a single line, as
she did in *The Unknown*, a spiritualistic play by Somerset
Maugham, which I was not lucky enough to see, when
she cried out, 'Who is going to forgive God?' And in an
undistinguished melodrama about Edmund Kean at Drury
Lane, during a scene in the green room at the theatre, the
double doors at the back of the stage were suddenly thrown
open and 'Mrs Garrick' was announced. Haidée Wright, in a
dark dress and simple bonnet entered, walking with an ebony
stick, and moving down to H. A. Saintsbury, who was

playing Kean, handed him a case which she was holding in her hand. As she opened it, she said very simply, 'Mr Kean, these are my husband's medals,' and the whole audience sat spellbound and tearful, although the episode was quite unconnected with the rest of the play.

With American audiences she was equally popular. The part of the old actress in *The Royal Family* (founded on the Barrymores by Kauffmann and Hart) was created in New York by Haidée Wright. In London the part was played by Marie Tempest, but I fancy that Haidée Wright's performance must have had a touch of the barnstormer which may have been broader and more colourful. Her voice, with its strange throbbing tremolo, became more mannered in her later years and it was easy to imitate her quavering tones. But I never liked to hear anyone make fun of her, and refused to go to see her in a stupid play, *The Aunt of England*, in which people said that she was beginning to caricature herself. When I came to know her personally I found that she suffered from poor health and a kind of persecution mania, complaining of being bullied by her directors and harassed by financial worries. 'Dear Haidée Wright,' said the witty Lady Tree, 'always so right, and never in her heyday.'

She told me once that her greatest youthful ambition had been to play Juliet, for which of course she never had the looks. In her earliest days in the theatre she had acted a boy's part in Wilson Barrett's famous religious melodrama, *The Sign of the Cross*, and learned to give blood-curdling screams from offstage as she was being tortured, and she was a painted lady of uncertain age in Forbes-Robertson's greatest commercial success, *The Passing of the Third Floor Back*, a wildly sentimental piece in which Christ, thinly concealed under the disguise of a character called 'The Stranger', arrived to persuade the guests in a Bloomsbury lodging house to abjure their selfish ways.

She was, I suppose, somewhat old-fashioned in her acting by the time I saw her, and I must reluctantly admit that in two modern plays, *The Distaff Side* by John Van Druten, and a drama adapted from the French called *No Man's Land* (in which she was a peasant mother forced to shoot her own son at the climax of the play) she did seem to be rather too blatantly stagey to be entirely convincing. Why was she never

given the opportunity, I wonder, to play Volumnia, Queen
Margaret or Hecuba? She would have been magnificent in
such roles, for she needed tragedy – and how few tragedians,
men or women, have we ever produced in the English theatre!
– to display her emotional powers to the full. She had a great
spirit in her little body, and the passionate intensity which
she could always evoke, even with indifferent material, revealed an iron discipline and technique as striking in the
actress as it was emotionally moving to the audience.

29

THREE BRILLIANT
ECCENTRICS

*ESMÉ PERCY, ERNEST THESIGER, AND
ROBERT FARQUHARSON*

They were all three very unusual in appearance for those
days – dandified, flamboyant, fond of wearing jewellery and
unconventional clothes. Thesiger was tall and angular, with
a long turned-up nose of a most unusual shape, Farquharson
thickset and slightly lame, with big pebble spectacles and
reddish-gold hair which appeared to be dyed, a face which
looked as if it were painted (and possibly was) and a congenital
stammer which disappeared when he was acting. Esmé Percy,
on the other hand, was short and plump, with a broken nose
and only one eye, disabilities which must have been horribly
painful to his vanity, but which he had learned to overcome
by sheer force of personality and charm. He lost his eye just
before the Second War, when he was attacked by a Great
Dane he was stroking. The accident upset him terribly and
he even contemplated suicide. But he always adored dogs and
kept one with him to the end, although he had twice been
seriously mauled by them. As a young man he had been a
great beauty but I never heard him bitter at growing old and
losing his looks. He even took it in good part, when, in *The
Lady's Not For Burning*, in which he was inimitably funny
as the drunken tinker in the last act, his false eye fell out on
to the stage. We were all too dismayed to move, until one of
the young men in the cast, who was also a doctor, managed

to step forward and surreptitiously hand it back to him. Meanwhile Esmé was heard to murmur, 'Don't step on it, for God's sake. They're so expensive!' After this episode, I suggested he might wear a black patch which suited the part very well, and somewhat reluctantly he agreed to do so. His sweetness over the affair was very typical. Sorting out some old letters written to me at various times about my acting, I found several from him which were among the most generous I ever received from a fellow-player.

He delighted in the company of young people, and when we took *The Lady* to America his enthusiasm was enchanting. Though already an elderly man, he would seek out the most interesting places to visit, and get himself elected to several of the best clubs in Washington, Boston, and New York, to which he took me as his guest, and insisted on giving supper parties in Greenwich Village, at which all the youngsters sitting round him were fascinated by his stories and the amusing comments with which he embellished them.

His mother was French, and Esmé used to boast that he had been trained in Sarah Bernhardt's company, and that she had advised him to leave it because he was too much like her. He gave a wonderful lecture about her in which he imitated her voice to perfection.

His own vocal range was extraordinary. Once, during the war, broadcasting with me in a radio version of *Hamlet*, he acted three parts, the Ghost, the Player King, and Osric, using a different pitch and tone of course for each. He played a great deal of Shaw, and revelled in the elaborate speaking of Shavian prose, though he was also a somewhat inaccurate study and the prompter was apt to be a good deal in evidence during his performances. I saw him in *The Shewing-up of Blanco Posnet,* and as Dubedat in *The Doctor's Dilemma* with Gwen Ffrangcon Davies.

At the end of the First World War when he ran a theatre in Cologne for the British troops, he persuaded Mrs Patrick Campbell to come out and appear with him in *Pygmalion*, when she proceeded to behave in her usual unpredictable fashion. Throughout the first act she kept muttering to Higgins, 'Oh, do get on. Get on. You're so slow.' In the second, as he tried to follow her instructions, she whispered, 'Now you're gabbling, you know. You're much too fast.'

And in the third, while he tremblingly awaited the final onslaught, she gazed down sadly at his suede shoes (considered a very unmanly fashion in those far-off days), and remarked, shaking her head sadly as she turned to him with her back towards the audience. 'Oh you're quite wrong. He's not that kind of man at all.'

ERNEST THESIGER

Ernest Thesiger too, was a splendid Shavian actor. His famous performance as the Dauphin in the original production of *Saint Joan*, with Sybil Thorndike, was definitive – an astonishing mixture of Gothic fantasy, brilliant comedy and underlying pathos. He later made successes in two other Shaw plays, *Geneva* – in which he wore an eyeglass and looked like Austen Chamberlain – and as Charles the Second in *In Good King Charles's Golden Days*, just before the Second War. During the Twenties, his ghillie in Barrie's *Mary Rose* failed to convince me, though he boasted of having taken long walks to Battersea Park with a real Scottish peasant whom he had hired to teach him the correct accent. But I thought he should never play anything but upper-class characters, though perhaps he might have been amusing as Malvolio, since he could appear very overweening when he chose. He was often waspish and sometimes malicious (though less so as he grew older) but he was also very courageous. He had joined up as a private soldier in the First War, refusing to take a commission, and was very popular with the other men, who were greatly impressed to see him sitting in a trench among them, busily engaged in doing needlework. His hands were badly scarred by shrapnel wounds, but he managed them admirably on the stage and was very proud of his hobbies, painting and petit-point. He was fond of collecting antiques and bibelots. These he would exhibit on a shelf in his dressing-room and would sometimes sell them to members of the company or give them as presents to his friends. He loved hobnobbing with Royalty, and liked to mention that Queen Mary and Princess Marie-Louise often showed a gracious interest in his work. He was thrifty about money and loved to sharpen his wit on that of his many witty contemporaries. He led the

Men's Dress Reform League at one time, and championed
shorts and more comfortable leisure clothes, swathing his
neck in scarves fastened with jewelled pins long before they
began to become a fashion. Somebody once asked him, 'What
do you say when you meet Nijinsky?' 'Oh,' replied Ernest
gravely, 'say? You don't say anything. You just give him a
pearl.' It was said that he always wore a string of very good
pearls round his own neck, and never took it off for fear that
the loss of the warmth of his skin might spoil their quality.
One night at the beginning of 1940 there was an air-raid
warning at Oxford, where he happened to be acting in a new
play, and was staying at the Randolph Hotel. All the guests
were ordered to go down to the basement shelter. Ernest
created somewhat of a sensation, vividly dressed in Russian
high-necked pyjamas and a spectacular dressing-gown, and
sat bolt upright in a corner with his spectacles on his nose and
a piece of embroidery in his hands. After a while the assembled
company began to doze and he knew he was no longer
attracting such conspicuous interest. Suddenly he clutched his
throat and cried, 'My God! My pearls! No, no, it's all right.
I've got them on.'

He played the first Witch for me in *Macbeth* during 1942,
and was very effective and uncanny in the part. He had always
a brilliant talent for female impersonation. One of the best
scenes in Noël Coward's first big Cochran Revue, *On With
The Dance*, was a boarding house sketch in which Thesiger
and Douglas Byng, as two old harridans, undressed as they
made ready for bed. And I once saw him give an impersonation of Violet Vanbrugh, whose striking looks he managed
to caricature most cleverly.

The last time he appeared in London we were together in
an unsuccessful play, and I met him one day in the street
shortly before we began rehearsing and said how glad I was
that he had promised to undertake the part. 'I think it is a
splendid play,' I said. 'Don't you?' 'I'm afraid I don't,' Ernest
murmured darkly and went his way. I didn't dare to ask him
why, in that case, he had agreed to accept the engagement,
but during the short run he acted with his usual distinction
and received quite an ovation from the audience at his entrance
on the first night. But he was tiring fast, and I used to feel
sad as I passed his open dressing-room door to see him

lying on the sofa half asleep between his scenes. He was an extraordinary and rather touching character, an actor of unique imagination, with a most beautiful perfection of speech and period style.

ROBERT FARQUHARSON

Robert Farquharson's real name was Robin de la Condamine, and he was reputed to be a rich amateur with a background of Italian nobility. He acted with Tree at His Majesty's and I was surprised to find his name, along with those of Granville-Barker and Courtenay Thorpe, in the cast list of the copyright performance of *Caesar and Cleopatra* given by Mrs Patrick Campbell in 1899, showing that he must have been touring with her at that time in some other play. I had often heard when I was a young man of his huge personal success as Herod in Wilde's *Salome*, given for a private performance, so when he came behind the scenes with a mutual friend after my extremely immature performance of Romeo to Gwen Ffrangcon Davies's Juliet (I was then only nineteen years old) I was extremely flattered to hear him say, 'You have taught me something about the part of Romeo I never knew before!' Unfortunately I boasted of the supposed compliment to the same mutual friend a few days later, and was shattered to be told, 'Robin said it was the first time he had ever realised that Romeo could be played as Juliet.'

It took a good many years for me to recover from this snub, and I was always slightly in awe of Farquharson whenever I happened to meet him. Once, standing in a crowded bus, he called out to me, peering through the heads and shoulders of the other passengers, 'I'm just off to see my d-d-darling d-d-dentist!' Though his acting was vivid and original, I always found it slightly out of key with the rest of the productions in which he played. In *Such Men Are Dangerous*, an adaptation by Ashley Dukes of a German play, he appeared as the mad Emperor Paul the First. I had acted in New York in the same play – then called *The Patriot* (with Lyn Harding, Leslie Faber and Madge Titheradge in the other leading parts) and it had failed completely and closed after only a few performances. But in London, given, as I thought, a much inferior production, with Isobel Elsom and Matheson Lang as the other two stars, the play achieved a considerable run. But Farquharson and Lang were reputed not to get on well together and I seemed to be aware of their disharmony, so that . their performances, though individually effective enough, failed to satisfy me. Still, Farquharson was always much in demand for highly-coloured characters, and Lewis Casson and Sybil Thorndike engaged him to play Iachimo in their production of *Cymbeline* and also Count Cenci in Shelley's tragedy, which they were adventurous enough to present for special matinées.

In the early Thirties he appeared as Cardinal Wolsey, with Flora Robson as Queen Katharine and Charles Laughton as Henry the Eighth, under Tyrone Guthrie's direction, at Sadler's Wells and the Old Vic. In 1968, when I was acting the part of Wolsey myself at the Old Vic (with Edith Evans as Katharine and Harry Andrews as the King). I was walking along the Kings Road, Chelsea one fine morning when I suddenly saw Farquharson perilously riding a bicycle among the heavy traffic. I waved to him rather timidly and was greatly surprised when he lightly vaulted off the bicycle and wheeled it on to the pavement. 'How are you, J-J-Jack?' he cried (no one had called me Jack since I first went on the stage in 1921). 'All right,' I answered, rather self-consciously. 'You know I'm trying to play your part in *Henry the Eighth*.' 'Oh yes,' he said, 'I know. We both made the s-s-same mistake. We ought to have padded ourselves and made ourselves look enormously f-f-fat. When I played it the whole production was geared to show off s-s-some film actor or other,[1] and, when I came on, the director lowered all the lights and wheeled an enormous s-s-s-sideboard on to the stage which extinguished me entirely.' So saying he guided his bicycle off the pavement, sprang into the saddle, and, in his green tweed suit and brown boots, disppeared among the tangle of cars and buses and was lost to me for ever.

[1] Charles Laughton

30

TWO EXQUISITE COMEDIENNES

DAME MARIE TEMPEST AND YVONNE ARNAUD

During the Twenties and Thirties there were perhaps half a dozen famous names prominently displayed in lights over the entrances of the theatres, though the plays might often prove to be of considerably less distinction than the players who adorned them. The fashionable little comedies of those days would often begin at half past eight or a quarter to nine, and, with two intervals, enlivened by a small and scratchy orchestra sawing away in the recesses of a tiny pit covered with imitation palm-leaves, the final curtain would often fall well before eleven o'clock. But the public seldom seemed to resent such scanty fare, especially when the names of Marie Tempest or Yvonne Arnaud twinkled in lights above the title of the play.

Both actresses were short and a little plump, but they were fascinating performers and played with inimitable inventiveness and style. With a wink here, a nod there, a giggle or a pout, absurd displays of temper or tears among the teacups, an expressive use of a tiny handkerchief, they could provoke or stifle laughter, point a line or repair a moment or two of emotional stress. Experts in phrasing and timing (both were trained musicians) they would take the stage like Millamant, 'sails spread, with a shoal of fools for tenders', the one with her short brisk steps and bristling with authority, the other bustling about with endearing liveliness and humour.

DAME MARIE TEMPEST

My first two meetings with Marie Tempest were somewhat intimidating occasions. At a smart lunch party at which I had been introduced to her for the first time, she suddenly announced that the strap which held her shoes had become undone and I was despatched to the host's bedroom to find a button-hook. Kneeling clumsily beneath the tablecloth I dug the implement fiercely into the curve of her instep and emerged covered with confusion. One afternoon, a few days later, as I was going round to see a member of her company, she suddenly appeared, veiled and cloaked, at the stage-door, impatient to get home for the evening rest which was such an important item in her inflexible routine. Hoping she might remember me, I crushed her tiny fingers brutally in what I hoped was a manly handshake, and thought I heard her mutter fiercely 'Blast you!' (though such an expression from such august lips seemed wildly improbable) as she plunged into her waiting car and was driven away.

When she created the part of the actress Judith Bliss in Noël Coward's *Hay Fever* in 1925 she immediately regained the enormous popularity which was to continue during the rest of her career. Her prestige had been somewhat in eclipse after she returned to London in 1922 from a World tour and, failing for several seasons to find a suitable vehicle for her talents, she was even forced to play some secondary parts. But she took these reverses in her stride and was soon rewarded with the play she needed. The young playgoers who saw her in *Hay Fever* for the first time marvelled at her grace and composure, her wit and technical skill, while her old admirers continued to praise her beautiful diction and phrasing (she had been trained as a singer by Garcia, and triumphed as a star in light opera during her early years), and to delight in the unfailing distinction with which she walked the stage or sat erect, with her tiny elegantly shod feet crossed in front of her, wearing beautifully cut clothes and (as Noël Coward used to say) one of her crisp little hats.

She was in Edwardian travelling dress when I saw her first,
acting in a revival of *Alice Sit By The Fire* – a sentimental
Barrie play which hardly suited her better than it had suited
Ellen Terry, for whom it was originally written – and on her
first entrance she appeared in a hat which seemed to consist
of an entire pheasant, with the beak standing guard above her
turned-up nose. The audience applauded vigorously, and she
came forward from the open doorway and smiled and bowed
her acknowledgments to left and right before beginning her
performance. This was the practice of all the great stars of
that period – Mrs Patrick Campbell, Irene Vanbrugh, Marion
Terry, Julia Neilson – though today we should certainly think
such behaviour very odd. On the first night of one of Milne's
light comedies the director had even thoughtfully provided a
large tray (set out on a sideboard with several vases of artificial
flowers) for Irene Vanbrugh to carry round the stage, putting
them down on various tables, in order to cover the tremendous applause which greeted her first entrance.

Marie Tempest was very fond of clothes, and wore them
to perfection. The short skirts of the Twenties suited her
extremely well, and she used to wear pearl stud earrings, one
black and one pink, if I remember rightly, and her hair was
discreetly tinted to reddish gold. She was meticulous in the
care of her stage dresses, always wore a light white cloak over
her costume in passing from her dressing-room to the stage,
and insisted that all the other ladies in the cast should do the
same. Once made up and dressed, she never sat down in her
dressing-room but stood on a white drugget, and so her
dresses were always fresh and seldom had to be replaced
during a long run. It was said that the new shoes ordered to
go with each dress were sent straight to her own house, and
she would bring old ones to wear in the play that were more
comfortable. On one occasion a rather emotional young
actress, who had been deservedly chidden for unpunctuality
and carelessness during a performance, flung herself at Marie
Tempest's feet to beg her pardon, but Dame Marie cut her
short with a toss of her head and the brusque command, 'Get
up! Get up! Have you no respect for your management's
clothes?'

She was a martinet, severe and didactic even to her friends,
and a demon of discipline in the theatre. But her bark was

worse than her bite. Her marriage to Graham Browne was an ideal partnership, and they had already lived devotedly together for many years before they were able to be married. Browne was a good actor – better sometimes than he was given credit for, as he always stood back to give the limelight to his wife – and a charming, modest man. He died during the run of a play in which they were, as usual, acting together. On the morning of the funeral Marie Tempest ordered her car and came downstairs in a summer frock, having first made sure that all the flowers and wreaths which filled the hall should be cleared away. She spent the morning rehearsing with her husband's understudy and appeared as usual at the evening performance, disregarding the inevitable criticisms of those who were unkind enough to accuse her of indifference and thought she should have closed the theatre.

She never appeared in the classics, though Sheridan and Congreve would surely have suited her stylishness to perfection. My father always compared her favourably with Rejane and Mrs Kendal (both of whom he admired enormously, though I never saw either of them on the stage myself) but both of these actresses had been equally accomplished mistresses of pathos as well as comedy. Much as I revelled in Marie Tempest's comic gifts, I always found her less convincing in the few dramatic scenes I saw her play. However, those who were lucky enough to remember a stage version of *Vanity Fair*, in which she made a big dramatic success as Becky Sharp, maintained that it was the fault of the playwrights that she was not provided with better opportunities to show the more serious possibilities of which she was capable. Her acting in two fine death scenes, both in the Kauffman and Hart *Theatre Royal*, in which she appeared with Madge Titheradge and Laurence Olivier, and in *Little Catherine*, a Russian melodrama from the French of Alfred Savoir which ran for a very few weeks and was only remembered for her fine performance in it, showed her to great advantage in contrast to her usual run of frivolous parts. But in *The First Mrs Fraser*, by St John Ervine, I overheard a rival actress sitting near me murmuring (with some fairness), 'Oh, I can't be very pleased with Mary for that,' as the curtain fell on an emotional scene.

Her Stage Jubilee took place at Drury Lane Theatre in 1937,

and I had the honour of being chosen to recite some verses introducing a great pageant of players marshalled by Tyrone Guthrie in her honour. Royalty was in a box, and Marie Tempest was carried on in a big gold chair, wearing a soft pink chiffon dress which floated round her as she made her faltering (but expert) little speech of thanks, curtseying first to the Queen and then to the audience, with her usual consummate grace. Then, after the curtain had finally fallen, she turned and bowed to us all, and, frail, tiny, but still immensely dignified, walked away to her dressing-room.

She continued acting for five years more with undiminished energy, both in London and on tour. She moved to a new flat and decorated her rooms, continued to buy bibelots, dinner services, presents, and to regulate her household with minute attention. From her dressing-room she would send for members of her company and lecture them individually, questioning them about their health, their love-affairs, and their behaviour generally, in private life as well as on the stage, and giving practical orders and advice. She was interested in every detail – in their diets, doctors, and dentists and the workings of their insides as well as in their acting.

I was with her when she created her last new role, the grandmother in Dodie Smith's *Dear Octopus*, produced on the eve of Munich. She behaved impeccably at rehearsals, though we were all a little afraid of her at first, but the young director, Glen Byam Shaw, handled her with perfect tact, and she listened to him obediently. She had some difficulty in learning her lines, and we were convinced that, except for her own part, she had never even read the play. 'Are those some of my children?' she would inquire doubtfully, as another of the large assembly of characters came forward to greet her. One day she sent us all away while she took a lesson to learn 'The Kerry Dances', two verses of which she was to sing in the nursery scene. When we returned some hours later she had mastered it with apparent ease, and sang it enchantingly at the cottage piano, her voice still sweet and true. In the last act I liked to watch her in the scene when she was folding napkins for a dinner party in the shape of water-lilies. She was supposed to have drunk a cocktail and was a little tipsy, throwing one of the napkins into the air and catching it just in time with a wicked chuckle.

We became great friends during the run. I would be invited every evening to go to her dressing-room during one of my waits. There, with the white drugget on the floor and the patience cards laid out (she always played patience every night when she arrived at the theatre) I would be given French bread and butter and a cup of coffee, served by her dresser-companion with impressive ceremony.

When we were in Newcastle to try out the play, Marie Tempest insisted on coming down every morning in the hotel, always beautifully dressed. Sometimes she wore a big shady straw hat with a gardenia decorating the brim, and she always turned back her white gloves over the wrists as she ate her lunch. Sometimes we would go for a short drive together before her afternoon rest, and it was amusing to watch her choosing a cock-lobster ('not a hen,' she stipulated firmly) after she had climbed in her high heels over a steep step into the little white-washed cottage where the woman who was selling the lobsters had her shop. The creatures were scuttling about all over the stone floor, but Marie Tempest went on calmly chattering to her and seemed to understand what she was saying, despite her very thick Northumbrian accent.

When the War broke out, *Dear Octopus* closed in London. Her Regent's Park flat was bombed, and she moved for a few weeks to Great Fosters, the hotel near Windsor, where I also happened to be staying for a few nights while I was making a film at Teddington. Here I would encounter her among the other residents, walking impatiently to and fro in the Great Hall during an air raid, impeccable as ever in a suit of blue slacks, and as a particularly loud explosion shook the walls I heard her remark to her companion, 'Quelle vie de dog!' (A rival actress was once heard to remark, 'Do you think Mary speaks what they call working French?')

My contract in *Dear Octopus* had expired and I left the play which had resumed its run after the blitz, but she continued acting in it for many months. Not long afterwards she was taken ill. I went to call on her with books and flowers, but after ten minutes' nervous conversation she caught me surreptitiously looking at my watch. 'It was sweet of you to come, my dear,' she said drily, 'but you think me rather an old bore really, don't you?' I felt deeply ashamed, for I loved and admired her very much. But a few days later, in October 1942, she was dead.

YVONNE ARNAUD

Yvonne Arnaud, like Marie Tempest, was a brilliant musician. She had been something of a prodigy as a child pianist, playing in public with big orchestras abroad. She then achieved great success on the stage in London, where she sang and danced in *The Girl in the Taxi*. This I never saw, but I well remember the coloured poster which advertised it – a man and a girl getting into a cab from opposite sides, 'Mine I think! Mine I believe!' 'Ours I hope!' She was delightful as Mrs Pepys in James Bernard Fagan's play, *And So To Bed*, after she had been leading lady in the splendid Aldwych farces with Ralph Lynn, Tom Walls, and Mary Brough. In the first of these, *Tons of Money*, she scored with a wonderfully funny gag-line at every crisis, 'Aubrey, I've got an idea,' delivered in her inimitable broken English. In *By Candle Light*, an adaptation from the Viennese, she was a perfect foil for Leslie Faber and Ronald Squire, but this success was sadly interrupted by Faber's sudden and untimely death.

When I first acted in New York, in 1928, she was playing next door with the English company of *And So To Bed*, and Emlyn Williams, then a young man of twenty-two, was in the cast. Emlyn and I would go off to speak-easies (knocking at the gratings of little doors and fearing we should be blinded by bath-tub gin) and Yvonne Arnaud was enchantingly kind to me whenever I was lucky enough to meet her.

Fifteen years later, during the Second War, when she had starred in a number of very slight comedies and carried most of them to success on her supremely capable shoulders, I remembered her performance as Mrs Pepys, and persuaded her to appear as Mrs Frail in a revival that I was planning of Congreve's *Love for Love*. There was some trouble over her costumes, for she could not wear the correctly tight corsets of the period as she had a weak chest and caught bronchitis and bad colds very easily. But she compromised with bones sewn into her bodices, and when, at the dress parade, she stepped on to the stage at the Opera House, Manchester (where we opened the play), spreading her fan and smoothing out her ample skirts, and remarked with a sly wink, 'Not so bad, do you think, for an old girl!' I was her devoted slave.

She would not sleep in London during air-raids but would send her dresser out to shop for her, rushing off to Waterloo as soon as the play was over laden with bags and parcels, and riding triumphantly in the guard's van of a train to reach her country house, coaxing smiles and friendly help from everyone on the way.

When she was ill for several weeks and unable to appear, the play suffered dreadfully without her. We all loved the way she shared our scenes with us, and the skill she could use to cover weaknesses if she was acting with a less accomplished performer than herself.

Her technique was as unfailing as her instinct. One might have supposed that the elaborate verbiage of Congreve would have proved something of a problem for her, with her French accent, after a lifetime of speaking modern colloquial dialogue, but she used her breathing and timing as cunningly as ever and rose to the challenge like a bird. She was the only leading actress I have ever known who looked forward to a first night with happy anticipation and really seemed to enjoy every single moment of it. She should of course have played in some of the Molière comedies and the farces of Feydeau. Best of all, what fun it would have been if one had ever been able to see her acting in a play with Marie Tempest!

31

THREE REMARKABLE
CHARACTER ACTORS

LESLIE FABER, SIR CEDRIC HARDWICKE,
CHARLES LAUGHTON

LESLIE FABER

Leslie Faber was a tall, distinguished-looking man with pale
blue eyes and a long upper lip. His fair hair, worn rather long
and streaked with grey when I knew him, was brushed in
wings round either side of his head. His clothes were dark
and conventional. Only his hats, worn at a jaunty angle, had
curly brims[1] and betrayed the actor. He somewhat resembled
the well-known portraits of George Washington, as the
American critics were quick to notice when he went to act in
New York. He was of Danish extraction, and a photograph of
him still hangs in the Theatre Museum at the Fredericksborg
Castle in Copenhagen. He was the first West End star to take
notice of me and encourage my early efforts as an actor, and
apart from that I was to grow deeply fond of him as a friend.

He was extremely successful in disguising himself and
evolving clever make-ups. As a mysterious Count in a play
called *In The Night* he peered from underneath a large top hat
and was enveloped in a huge overcoat with a fur collar. As

---

[1] Though not as curly as the hats worn by Allan Aynesworth, which
were always strikingly individual.

the Scottish police doctor (who turned out to be the criminal when they finally solved the mystery) in Edgar Wallace's *The Ringer*, he had a square bowler, a red nose, baggy trousers and shabby boots, and sucked endless cigarettes, holding them, between puffs, in curled mittened fingers. But it was in *Jane Clegg*, a gloomy kitchen-sink drama by St John Ervine, that his acting first made a great impression on me, though I remember little of the play itself. His part was that of a drunken idle husband, nagging and bullying his long-suffering wife (Sybil Thorndike) and his crotchety old mother-in-law (Clare Greet, a fine old actress who had created Shaw's Rummy Mitchens in *Major Barbara* and the charwoman in *Outward Bound*). But he was splendid too in straight parts, and I greatly admired his performances in various melodramas – *Havoc, The Outsider, White Cargo, The Sign on the Door*, and Maugham's *The Letter*, in all of which he acted with power, sensitivity, and taste. But his greatest success proved ironically to be his last. He went into management with Ronald Squire, and they presented together a delightful comedy, *By Candle Light*, in which Leslie Faber as the Baron and Squire as his valet acted the two leading parts, with Yvonne Arnaud, at her enchanting best, as a *soubrette* maid. But Faber was working too hard, filming during the day as well as acting in the theatre every night, and he caught pneumonia after a week-end cruise on a boat he had just bought to celebrate the success of the play, and died after only a short illness.

He had always longed to succeed in romantic parts, but there was something austere in his personality which stood in his way. He could convey sensuality but not great warmth. His natural hauteur must have been effective when he played Jason to Sybil Thorndike's Medea, but apparently he failed when he played Shakespeare's Richard the Second for some special Sunday night performance. He must have invited me to watch a rehearsal, for I have a vivid recollection of him sitting in a big chair, dressed in a dark business suit, with a Homburg hat tilted over one eye for a crown, and an incongruous sceptre held in the crook of his arm, but I never saw him play the part, though he told me afterwards that he had failed to please himself in it. I found in him, as in many fine actors, a strange mixture of vanity, confidence, and self-dissatisfaction. He could be extremely generous, and was always enchantingly kind both to me and my brother Val (who was understudying and walking-on in *The Ringer* when he first met him) but he could also be narrow-minded, bitter and suspicious, and I think he felt he had never achieved the position to which his talents should have entitled him.

He wore period costume with ease, and was a fine Macduff in a very bad production of *Macbeth* in which the American star, James Hackett, appeared with Mrs Patrick Campbell. He would, I am sure, have been an ideal Joseph Surface, but I do not think he ever played the part. He was also a most talented director, and I was lucky enough to work under him on two occasions for special performances in the early Twenties. I was already secretly cherishing an ambition to direct a play myself, and watched with admiration the way in which Faber handled the authors and players under his control, making tactful but important adjustments in the texts, and illuminating the action by the way in which he arranged the entrances and exits and the disposition of the characters.

In the second of these Sunday productions he acted the leading part himself as well as directing the play, a romantic costume melodrama called *Huntersmoon* (adapted I think from the Danish) in which my second cousin, Phyllis Neilson-Terry, who had given me my first professional engagement in 1921, played the heroine, and I was cast as her cowardly husband. Faber's part was a kind of Sydney Carton character, secretly in love with the heroine for whom he sacrificed his life in the last act. He was modest enough to ask me what I thought of his performance, and I ventured to say that I thought he should take the stage more boldly and sweep the audience off their feet in the manner of my great-uncle Fred Terry, Phyllis's father. But he smiled sadly and said he only wished he could act like that.

In 1928 he went, with Lyn Harding and Madge Titheradge, to New York, to appear for Gilbert Miller in a German play, *The Patriot*, translated and adapted by Ashley Dukes. A young actor playing the Tsarevitch proved inadequate and Faber cabled suggesting me as a substitute. I sailed immediately and arrived in time for the dress-rehearsal, having learnt my short but effective part on board ship. But New York would have none of the play and we sadly returned to London after only ten days' run.

In the following year, Faber invited me to go with him to see the English production of the same play, re-named *Such Men Are Dangerous*, with Matheson Lang in the leading part. We both felt the later version to be inferior to the one in which we had appeared in America, but Lang was a great favourite in London, and achieved considerable personal success. He was a fine actor too, less subtle, to my mind, than Leslie, but with greater sex-appeal.

When Faber died, the obituary notices gave a long list of his successful appearances and praised his fine career, but I always felt that his somewhat cynical manner covered an unhappy personal life and a deep sense of disappointment even with the work he loved so well.

SIR CEDRIC HARDWICKE

Cedric Hardwicke was not unlike Faber in some respects – the same long upper lip and slightly sardonic reserve. He was somewhat forbidding in straight parts, but could be very endearing when he was able to disguise his appearance and create odd characters quite unlike himself. He was superb as Churdles Ash in *The Farmer's Wife* and in *Yellow Sands*, two Eden Philpotts comedies in which he scored enormous personal successes, and he was always good in Shaw – as the He-Ancient in *Back to Methuselah*, as Caesar (with Gwen Ffrangcon Davies as Cleopatra), as Shotover in *Heartbreak House* and Magnus in *The Apple Cart* with Edith Evans. He was the Gravedigger in the first modern-dress Shakespearean production, with Colin Keith-Johnson as the Prince (it was christened 'Hamlet in Plus Fours'), and of course I was greatly impressed by his performance as the hateful incestuous Father in *The Barretts of Wimpole Street*, again opposite Gwen Ffrangcon Davies. His manner in this part was very subtly sinister, the mouth drawn down at the edges in a hypocritical sneer, with pious looks to Heaven as he made Henrietta swear on the Bible or forced Elizabeth to drink the mug of porter, and the pouting of his sensual lips as he ordered the dog to be destroyed.[1]

[1] I attempted the same role in a film remake of the play in 1958, and felt I was able to do little justice to the part.

His voice was rather dry and thick, but he used it with admirable effect in dialect and light comedy, though I think he did not have the range for tragic parts. A season with the Old Vic Company at the New Theatre, when he played Gaev to Edith Evans's Madame Ranevsky in *The Cherry Orchard*, and also Sir Toby Belch, with great success, was spoilt for him by an ill-fated production in which he was persuaded to appear as Faustus in Marlowe's tragedy. He had a long and distinguished career in films, both in England and California, but in his last years he seemed to lose heart and to break little fresh ground either in the cinema or the theatre.

We worked together only once, in Laurence Olivier's film of *Richard the Third*, and Ralph Richardson, one of his oldest and dearest friends, was also in the cast as Buckingham. Cedric Hardwicke seemed terribly depressed during our days together in the studio, and we all tried to cheer him up. 'I'm too old for this Shakespeare business,' he would say. I asked him what he was planning to do next, 'Oh,' he said, 'I have to go back to California to play Moses in *The Ten Commandments* and Louis the Eleventh in a musical of *If I were King*.' 'Good parts?' I asked. 'Oh Heaven knows,' said Hardwicke gloomily, 'my agent reads the scripts for me. I would never agree to do them if I had to choose them for myself.'

In his last success in the theatre he played, in New York, a Japanese gentleman in a light comedy, *The Majority of One*, starring with a well-known Jewish comedienne, Gertrude Berg. I was acting at a theatre nearby in *Much Ado About Nothing* with Margaret Leighton, and we would both dine with Cedric between performances on matinée days at Sardis, where he seemed happy to be with us and chattered delightfully on all sorts of topics. But we both felt that he was lonely and only the shadow of his former self. Like Faber, he had unhappy marriages and lost most of the money he had made in his most successful years. He spent his last months living alone in a hotel and died quite soon afterwards. He always seemed to be vaguely surprised at having received his knighthood and the high esteem in which he was held in his profession. I always loved Hardwicke's own story of being knighted by George the Fifth, who was deaf, and the King, prompted by a whisper from his equerry, saying, 'Rise, Sir Samuel Pickwick.' I should have liked to have known him better and perhaps been able to show him more sympathy and encouragement at a time when he must have needed them so badly.

CHARLES LAUGHTON

Cedric Hardwicke and Leslie Faber were both, I think, well aware of their physical and vocal limitations. Charles Laughton, who, despite a brilliantly versatile career, was more successful (first in the theatre and afterwards on the screen) than either of the other two, never achieved a real triumph in the parts he most longed to play. At the Old Vic he acted Macbeth with little success, insisted on choosing the part of Prospero rather than Caliban, in which he should have been superb, and never tackled Falstaff, a character for which in many ways he would surely have been ideally suited. Although he triumphed in Korda's film, *The Private Life of Henry the Eighth*, he made no great impact when he appeared as Shakespeare's Henry at Sadler's Wells and the Vic under Tyrone Guthrie, though his magnificent Angelo in *Measure for Measure*, and his Lopakhin in *The Cherry Orchard* during the same season, were unforgettably fine performances. His film creation of Captain Bligh in *Mutiny on the Bounty* was to bring him world-wide recognition[1], but his return to the theatre was less successful when, after a long absence, he appeared in Brecht's *Galileo* and as Undershaft in Shaw's *Major Barbara* (under Orson Welles's direction) in New York, and came back to appear at Stratford as Bottom and King Lear, and in London in a play called *Party*, when he was theatrical godfather to the young Albert Finney. He had become something of a legend in California, where he trained pupils, gave readings from the Bible and the classics, and took part in a famous reading of the 'Don Juan in Hell' scene from Shaw's *Man and Superman* with Cedric Hardwicke, Charles Boyer, and Agnes Moorehead. He was already ill before he returned to Los Angeles, where he died not long afterwards – in 1962.

In the early Twenties, when he suddenly burst on London,

---

[1] He also played Moulton-Barrett in *The Barretts of Wimpole Street* with great success in the first film version of the play with Norma Shearer and Frederic March.

his talent and versatility had taken the town by storm. He arrived from Yorkshire with a scholarship to the RADA, where Alice Gachet, a very perceptive teacher, coached him in some scenes in French, and at once became convinced of his great potential talent. Soon afterwards he was engaged for a part in Molnar's *Liliom* with Fay Compton, but the play failed completely. (It was the second version to be done in London, and equally unsuccessful on both occasions, though in New York the Theatre Guild had one of its first successes with it, starring Joseph Schildkraut and Eva le Gallienne, and later the musical version *Carousel* was to be enormously popular.) At the Duke of York's Theatre in London it was directed by Komisarjevsky, who, with his usual perversity, undertook the production, although he thoroughly disapproved of the casting of Fay Compton and Ivor Novello in leading parts. Charles Laughton, however, in a minor role (the apache friend of the hero) scored an immediate personal triumph, and shortly afterwards was to be seen, again under Komisarjevsky's direction, at the Barnes Theatre, as Solyony, the sinister officer with the scent-bottle in *The Three Sisters*, and as Epihodov in *The Cherry Orchard*. He was soon in demand in the West End where he acted in a series of plays of many different kinds. He appeared as the beaming detective Poirot in Agatha Christie's *Alibi*, and gave a sensational melodramatic performance as a Chicago gangster (derived from Al Capone) in Edgar Wallace's *On The Spot*, and a fascinating study of a seedy murderer in *Payment Deferred* which he later repeated on the screen.

Laughton, as I knew him in those early days, was an amiable mixture of boyish gaiety, moodiness, and charm. When he was first married to Elsa Lanchester they had a tree-house in the country, where they used to spend week-ends, and in London they lived in a charming flat in Gordon Square. I remember going to a party there. The big sitting-room had double doors, decorated with paintings of animals by the designer John Armstrong. Round the walls were low open bookshelves, lit from underneath, while on the glass shelves which ran along the top of them were specimen vases, filled with sprigs of blossom and single branches of foliage, which they had brought back from the country and arranged with exquisite taste.

I never knew Laughton very well. His acting did not rely on mimicry and I was greatly struck with the way in which, in spite of his own extraordinary individuality, he always seemed able to sink himself completely in a new part and find new colours and different ranges of voice for the characters he played. His old senator with the Southern accent in the film *Advise and Consent*, made very late in his career, was marvellously detailed and convincing.

His personality was as flexible as his appearance. He could be boyishly attractive or decadently sinister, with a menacing quality that might have made him a fine interpreter of Pinter. When he was cast as Worthing in *The Importance of Being Earnest* in his Old Vic Season, Tyrone Guthrie thought him so unpleasant that he took the part away from him and persuaded him to play Dr Chasuble, the oily rector, instead. But I always admired his courage in revealing the sensual side of his nature with such honesty and power. In the part of Angelo he trod the stage like an evil bat, with the billowing silk sleeves of his black gown flapping round him as he prowled up and down the stage, and he had immense drive, with a strong vein of poetic imagination which gave his performances colour and excitement. One might say, perhaps, that whereas Faber and Hardwicke were highly skilled dyed-in-the-wool professionals, Laughton was an inspired amateur. The first two men were perfectionists, calculating their acting to a nicety, and both struck me as being basically modest men, dry, witty, cynical. Laughton was more of an exhibitionist. His monsters were vicious with a kind of childlike *naïveté* fascinating in its contradictions. In *Macbeth* he made a sensation only in the Banquet Scene when confronted with the Ghost of Banquo, while in *King Lear* his scene on Dover Cliff made the greatest impression. He could not find and sustain the progression necessary to achieve either of these great parts to the full. How often stage and screen, dividing the loyalties of talented actors, have played havoc with their sense of direction and crippled their potentialities in consequence.

32

A BRILLIANT LEADING LADY

GERTRUDE LAWRENCE

Theatre audiences (and women especially), are apt to waste a great deal of time speculating on the ages of the actresses they have come to see. At the opening of a new revue at Manchester, for instance, I once sat behind two ladies who wrangled over the possible ages of Beatrice Lillie and Madge Elliott all through the interval, as well as whispering continually during the performance on the same absorbing topic. But Gertrude Lawrence was such a mercurial creature that the question of her age never occurred to one when she was acting, and when she died at the peak of her career in September 1952, her public and fellow players on both sides of the Atlantic were equally shocked, and the lights outside the theatres both on Broadway and in London were lowered to pay tribute to her memory.

I was never lucky enough to act with her, but once when we were both appearing in New York (she with Noël Coward in *Tonight at 8.30* and I in *Hamlet*), we were asked to take part in a great Midnight Charity Ball at the Astor Hotel. Gertrude Lawrence, as 'Day', was led into the ballroom on a large white horse. It was a very broad-beamed animal and she gave one look at it and remarked, 'A few inches wider and I shan't be able to make the matinée tomorrow.' As 'Night', I bestrode an equally imposing black steed. Our costumes had been specially designed by James Reynolds, a distinguished theatre-artist of the day, and I wore a helmet with long plumes and imposing-looking boots, though I only discovered at the last moment that they had thin paper soles, making it very difficult for me to mount and dismount with reasonable dignity. We were conducted on horseback all round the room, glancing somewhat apprehensively at the slippery floor, and were greeted with polite applause. Our mounts were then led away, and we took our places on two thrones facing each other, where we sat gazing at the back of Gipsy Rose Lee as she performed an elegant strip-tease, while the Honourable Thelma Furness, as the 'Sun', wearing a golden crown with large spiky rays attached to it, surveyed the scene from above us on another throne. Once the ceremony was over however we were completely forgotten by everyone, and we found ourselves standing rather forlornly together at the bar, drinking gin and tonics with our dressers and glad to slip away immediately afterwards.

Noël Coward has always said that Gertrude Lawrence's instinct was so incredibly quick and true that she ought to be sent home after the first reading of a new play and not be allowed to reappear until the first performance. She was always full of mischief, and incredibly versatile and unpredictable, even in private life. She was declared bankrupt while she was trying out a play in Manchester, and her financial affairs were usually in disorder, but this did not deter her from gaily ordering her flat to be redecorated or commissioning a new Rolls-Royce to be specially built for her, though quite forgetting to pay some small outstanding laundry bill.

She had beautiful jewels and was excessively generous. Edward Molyneux had given her *carte blanche* on condition that he provided her with her entire wardrobe, yet she could not resist sneaking off and buying dresses from other houses. She was apt to assume a different role on different days – the great Star, the Mother figure, the Cockney guttersnipe (she was Eliza Doolittle in Shaw's play in New York, and I would have given much to have seen her play it) or the industrious, approachable actress – all presented with equal skill and charm.

Her greatest fault (according to Coward who had many rows with her about it) was to embroider her performance after a few weeks with improvisations and funny business which sometimes spoiled the clean line of her otherwise brilliant readings. She had a seemingly effortless technique.

Her features were irregular, with a strange blob of a nose, but she had beautiful eyes and hands, wore clothes like a dream, and danced with exquisite grace. Although her voice was never very good (she wobbled if she had to sustain a high note and was frequently out of tune) she had learned to use it with beguiling charm.

In 'Fallen Babies', a sketch in Charlot's Revue (produced at the same time as Coward's play *Fallen Angels*) she and Beatrice Lillie were wheeled on to the stage in a huge double pram, with large rubber teats in their mouths. I think they drank cocktails too and chattered together in racy terms. I have two other favourite memories of her in Coward's first revue *London Calling* – one a monologue (which she played sitting up in a large bed, talking on the telephone to various friends in different voices) in which she was supposed to be a chorus-girl called Poppy Baker – the other, 'Parisian Pierrot', a song which she made nostalgically romantic, lying on a sofa of coloured cushions wearing black pyjamas. In another revue she was a slinky Chinese girl singing 'Limehouse Blues'. She could be fashionable, pathetic or broadly comic in successive scenes, changing from one mood to another without the slightest appearance of effort. Her forgetful hostess in Coward's *Hands Across The Sea* was hilariously funny, but she was equally brilliant half-an-hour later as the slatternly wife in *Fumed Oak*, eating a disgusting-looking bloater and picking the fish bones from between her teeth.

It was in revue and musical comedy that she had her greatest triumphs, though she also carried some rather indifferent straight comedies to success, and acted once in a serious drama of John Van Druten's *Behold We Live*, in which she starred with Gerald du Maurier. She appeared in a number of films (*Rembrandt* with Charles Laughton was one of them) but she was, I imagine, not easy to photograph and the medium did not greatly suit her. I always wondered whether she might not have been fascinating as Lady Teazle or as Beatrice, but she never ventured further than Shaw in the classic field. I once spent an afternoon trying to persuade her to play Sophy Fullgarney in a revival of Pinero's *The Gay Lord Quex* but though she seemed interested I do not think she ever found time to read the play. But I am happy to think I saw her in *The King and I* in New York only a few months before her death, waltzing enchantingly round the stage with Yul Brynner in her billowing white satin crinoline. She was a fascinating enigmatic creature, and the gramophone records she left behind, especially the famous scene with Coward in *Private Lives* and another in which she sings some of her best songs, remain to evoke something of her personality for the present generation as well as for those of us who had the joy of seeing her on the stage.

33

TWO FORCEFUL ACTORS

ROBERT LORAINE AND CLAUDE RAINS

ROBERT LORAINE

Loraine was a powerful, expressive actor, broadshouldered and possessed of a noble presence and a deep resonant voice. I thought his Cyrano perfection, and was greatly moved by his performance of Strindberg's *The Father* at the Everyman Theatre in the Twenties. I had also seen him as the young Australian soldier in Barrie's *Mary Rose* with Fay Compton at the Haymarket, and as Mirabell, to the definitive Millamant of Edith Evans, in *The Way of the World* when Nigel Playfair presented it at the Lyric, Hammersmith, but thought him a little heavy-handed for young romantic parts.

Shaw, who had saved him from drowning once when they were on a bathing expedition together, was always fond of him, and he was a splendid Bluntschli in *Arms and The Man* (in a revival charmingly designed by Hugo Rumbold) and had achieved great success as John Tanner in *Man And Superman* both in England and America. I gather from various hints in letters that Shaw would have liked him to create the part of Higgins in the first production of *Pygmalion*, but that Mrs Campbell firmly put her foot down. From my own slight personal experience of his behaviour and a considerable knowledge of her, I can well imagine that they would have been uneasy partners.

In 1927 I was asked to appear as Cassio to Loraine's Othello,
for a Sunday night and Monday matinée, by the Fellowship
of Players, with Ernest Thesiger as Roderigo, Ion Swinley as
Iago, Gertrude Elliott (Lady Forbes-Robertson, Sir Johnston's
widow) as Emilia, and Elissa Landi as Desdemona. Nobody
was paid, of course, but actors and actresses would gladly
play for the Sunday Societies in those days as a change from
long runs, or in the hope of strengthening their technique
and reputations if they were out of work.

James Whale (who directed the original *Journey's End* for
the Stage Society and was to win fame as a film director
in Hollywood not long afterwards) was in charge of the
rehearsals. He was an old friend of mine from my days in
J. B. Fagan's repertory theatre at Oxford. Every morning we
would begin to rehearse without Othello, but some twenty
minutes later Loraine, in a mackintosh and bowler hat, would
breeze into the theatre and, regardless of us all, proceed to
deliver the speech to the Senate from the centre of the stage,
forcing our little group to abandon our efforts and huddle
bashfully in the wings.

He listened to no one, least of all to the director, but made
an exception in the case of Lady Forbes-Robertson, for whose
advice he would occasionally ask. She brought along her
husband's prompt-book, and Loraine, finding the epilepsy
scene had been cut by the great man in his production, decided
immediately that he would not play it either. Elissa Landi
tried to protest at his violence as he strangled her in the final
scene, but he quickly silenced her with a pillow, remarking
firmly, 'You mind your own business, my dear young lady,
and I'll mind mine.'

At the dress-rehearsal he kept us all waiting for nearly an
hour while he indulged in a violent tantrum over his wig and
costume, and later sent strict instructions to us all to quit the
stage after the first company curtain at the end of the play so
that he might take a call alone. At the actual performance he
shooed us off like chickens and drew himself up in his robes
to acknowledge his reception. I could not help smiling, as I
stood in the wings, to see that Swinley (always the most
enchantingly modest of men both on and off the stage) had
braved the lightning by refusing to budge, and as the curtain
had already gone up, Loraine could only blink at him furiously

and pretend that he was only too delighted to share the honours with him after all.

The temperament of Othello may have been partly to blame on this occasion for such autocratic behaviour, though I think he was always a man of violent feeling. Edith Evans, however, told me that she greatly enjoyed acting with him in *The Way of the World* (they were together in another play, *Tiger Cats*, a sensational melodrama of no great account), and said he had once given her an excellent piece of advice. Beside the little Hammersmith theatre was a narrow alley, and the ragamuffins of the neighbourhood, who had nothing better to do, would knock with sticks and boots on the iron shutter of the scene dock, rattling and banging while the performance was going on and ruining the concentration of the actors. Loraine, however, turned to Edith Evans and remarked, 'If something in the theatre is troublesome, and can possibly be put right, it is perfectly legitimate to make a fuss. Otherwise you had best ignore it and get on with your work.'

But he could hardly have been able to ignore the situation when, on the first night of his revival of *Cyrano* in London, the stage-hands, resenting his rude treatment of them at the dress rehearsals, deliberately omitted to fasten the cleats holding up the stage tree under which Cyrano has to sit in the final scene, and the poor actor was forced to hold up the sagging piece of scenery with his back and finish the play as best he could.

CLAUDE RAINS

He had been callboy at His Majesty's Theatre under Tree, but by the time I first met him in the Twenties he was already much in demand as a successful character actor. He lacked inches and wore lifts in his shoes to increase his height. Stocky but handsome, with broad shoulders and a mop of thick brown hair which he brushed over one eye, he wore beautifully cut double-breasted suits, starched shirts with pointed collars with big cuffs, and wide satin ties. He had piercing dark eyes and a beautiful throaty voice, though he had, like Marlene Dietrich, some trouble with the letter 'R'. Extremely attractive to women, he was divorced several times, and once appeared (as Falkland in *The Rivals*) with Beatrix Thomson, to whom he was then married, in a cast that included two of his former wives. Needless to say, all the girls in my class at the Royal Academy of Dramatic Art, where he was one of the best and most popular teachers, were hopelessly in love with him.

I found him enormously helpful and encouraging to work with and was always trying to copy him in my first years as an actor, until I decided to imitate Noël Coward instead. As I understudied them both at different times, I suppose this was only to be expected. Rains, as Dubedat in *The Doctor's Dilemma*, was just the romantic boyish figure that I hoped to be, whether in his blue painter's smock sketching the doctors, or in the death scene, when he was wheeled on to the stage wrapped in a purple dressing-jacket with a rug over his knees, and his hands, made-up very white, hanging down over the arms of his chair.

He acted another artist, a sculptor this time, dying of morphine addiction, in a melodrama *Daniel* adapted from the French of Louis Verneuil. The part had been originally written for Sarah Bernhardt, who was seen in it during her last season in London. Though her leg had been amputated and she was over seventy, she contrived to give a remarkable effect of youth, and even masculinity, as she lay dying on a studio couch covered with rugs.

In the English version, Rains was extremely effective (Edith Evans, playing a silly mother in a white wig, who was always taking pills in the first act, was also in the cast), and a year or two later I was actually engaged myself to appear in the same character in an adaptation of the story for the cinema. This was my first silent film, with Isobel Elsom, Henry Vibart, and Mary Rorke, and it was shot at Teddington in very hot weather. I tried to emote with suitable abandon, encouraged by music played 'live' on a violin and piano in the film studio and a director who urged me on to absurdly melodramatic heights. In 1921 Nigel Playfair engaged me for my first London appearance in *The Insect Play* by the brothers Capek. He was to direct it at the Regent Theatre, King's Cross (later a cinema but now pulled down), and of course I was thrilled to be engaged for a professional appearance while I was still in my last term as a student at the Academy. Claude Rains led the cast, acting three different parts with his usual versatility, and when the play failed after only a few weeks, Playfair kept me on to appear in John Drinkwater's *Robert E. Lee*. In this play I was to be Lee's aide-de-camp – a very small part in which I had to follow Felix Aylmer about the stage, gazing through my fieldglasses at a good many rows of empty seats through several weeks of a hot summer, and tripping over my sabre in a long military overcoat. I also understudied Rains, who was playing the juvenile lead in the play, and took over from him for a few performances, gaining some confidence from the ordeal, though I imagine I was merely giving a tentative copy of the way I thought he played the part.

But though he won praise from the critics for several years in plays of many different kinds, Rains never achieved a big star position in London. He finally left England to follow a long and distinguished career on Broadway and afterwards in Hollywood, where his first success was, somewhat ironically, as The Invisible Man. 'I can't eat my notices,' he once said to me rather sadly, just before he went away. He acted with striking virtuosity and the London stage suffered a great loss when he deserted it for ever.

34

REMARKABLE HOSTESSES

LADY COLEFAX AND LADY CUNARD

I doubt if either of these two ladies would have been pleased to see their names bracketed together during their lifetime, for they were rivals in similar fields. Although they visited each other's houses and knew a great number of the same people, they were not at all similar in character. Some of their guests may have been inclined to be malicious at their expense, but few refused their invitations. Both of them collected lions, political, literary, and theatrical. Both had beautiful houses, and great taste in arranging their rooms, were experts at mixing the various celebrities they entertained, and adept at sparking off lively conversation.

LADY COLEFAX

It was said that Sibyl Colefax had founded her career as a successful hostess by inviting H. G. Wells and Bernard Shaw (on postcards) separately, declaring that each was eager to make the acquaintance of the other. At any rate she soon achieved a great reputation as a party-giver. She lived for many years at Argyll House, Chelsea, next door to another of her social rivals, Mrs Somerset Maugham, herself an energetic and talented hostess, destined in later years to compete with Lady Colefax as a professional decorator.

The panelled rooms at Argyll House were deliciously scented, and all the latest books – novels, biographies, and poetry – were heaped on a big low table in the drawing-room. There were always beautiful flowers, and the food and drink were perfect without the least display of ostentation. Lady Colefax was a small woman, though not as small as Lady Cunard, who resembled a brilliant canary, with curiously chiselled pale blue eyes. Both ladies were restless and indefatigable. Lady Colefax would think nothing of spending a week-end in the Isle of Wight, driving from Southampton next morning to lunch in Essex, before returning to London to give a party in the evening of the same day. Her car was always full of new books and stationery, so that she could keep abreast of her reading, or scrawl letters and postcards to her friends, both in England and America, in her almost illegible handwriting.

When she first invited me to supper at Argyll House I was naturally impressed to meet so many well-known people, most of whom I had only known before from their photographs in the newspapers. Gertrude Lawrence was to be an important guest on this occasion, but she was very late in arriving, and we sat down to supper without her. At last she was announced, and appeared in the doorway, looking as glamorous as she did on the stage. As she greeted Lady Colefax, she glanced round the supper table, and, seeing a young man seated on my left, sank to the ground in a deep curtsey, thinking him to be the Duke of Kent. Unfortunately he turned out to be a columnist from the *Daily Express*, but neither Lady Colefax or Miss Lawrence turned a hair. I only went once or twice to Argyll House, as Lady Colefax could no longer afford to live there, and she moved to Lord North Street, Westminster, just before the War, to a much smaller but equally charming house, and opened her decorating business in Brook Street with John Fowler as her partner. However she still continued to entertain with undiminished enthusiasm all through the War and for some years afterwards, when I grew to know her more intimately and became extremely fond of her. During the long painful illness which finally led to her death she stubbornly refused to give up her love of parties, and I found myself one day lunching in her dining room with a group of ten people, though she herself lay ill upstairs, and we were each of us asked to spend a few minutes with her before we left the house. She was faithfully

looked after to the end by the two maids who had been with
her for many years and ministered to her and to her guests
with unfailing tact and sweetness. Only a few weeks before
she died I had met her, walking with a stick and sadly bowed,
in the beautiful White Garden at Sissinghurst Castle where
she was staying with Harold Nicolson and his wife, Vita
Sackville-West. We sat down to a big schoolroom tea before
we left, with buns and cake and bread and butter – Nicolson
(wearing a big straw hat with the brim turned down all round)
at one end of the table, and his wife, in boots and breeches,
presiding at the other with a large brown teapot in her hand.

LADY CUNARD

Her real christian name was Maud, but she disliked it and
was always known as Emerald, though I never heard people
call her so to her face. She was American, but soon became
an important figure in London, though she had hunted
in Leicestershire when she first came to live in England with
her rich husband, Bache Cunard. Her two most intimate
and famous friends were George Moore and Sir Thomas
Beecham. She was extremely intelligent, amusing, and elegant, as well as being forthright and eagerly inquisitive. She
liked to refer to homosexuals as 'popinjays', and delighted to
fling challenging remarks at her guests on every kind of topic
as she sat at the head of her table. She had spent large sums
of money as a patroness of opera and ballet seasons at Covent
Garden and Drury Lane before the First War, and one always
met musicians and dancers, as well as writers and politicians,
at her parties. Until the Second War she lived in a large house
in Grosvenor Square, but I only went there once or twice.
She sold the house and went back to America, returning in
1944, when she established herself in a suite at the Dorchester
Hotel, where she continued to live until her death, surrounded
by her own beautiful impressionist pictures, books, and furniture. During this period I dined with her there a number of
times, and often took her to the theatre, of which she was
passionately fond, when I was not working myself. We would
go by taxi through the blackout to the Chantecler Theatre
near Gloucester Road, where Peter Brook was directing his

first productions in London of Cocteau's *Infernal Machine* and Ibsen's *John Gabriel Borkman*, and I once spent an evening with her sitting on a very hard uncomfortable pew at a church off Regent Street, watching a semi-professional performance of *Everyman*. She slept very little and read voraciously, Greek and Latin classics and poetry as well as contemporary books. She was always punctual and had beautiful manners. Her coquetry had something of the eighteenth century about it, and she entered or left a room with a brisk authority that reminded me of Marie Tempest.

I cherish one of her best remarks, an example of what we used to refer to, in a vanishing age of class distinction, as 'tumbril talk'. It was at one of her supper-parties at the Dorchester. The waiter looked rather sulky at being kept up late, though it was only about half past nine. Lady Cunard had been, as usual, to the theatre, and had invited nine or ten people to join her afterwards. It was the time of the V-2s, which everybody pretended to ignore, though it was impossible not to notice their whining as they went over. It was remarkable how audiences (and actors too) refused to allow the noise to interfere with performances in the theatres. As we sat down Lady Cunard gave a glance round the table and called the Head waiter to her side. 'Where is the butter?' she demanded. 'Butter, my lady,' said the man. 'I'm afraid there is no butter.' 'No butter?' said Lady Cunard. 'One must have butter. What is the Merchant Navy doing?' At that moment a V-2 exploded on the other side of the park with a hideous crash, but Lady Cunard did not even appear to have heard it.

I should like to have been able to write something of two other distinguished patronesses of the Arts, but I can only claim a very slight acquaintance with either of them. After the First World War, my eldest brother Lewis went back to Magdalen College, Oxford, invalided from the army. One of his greatest friends, from their earlier Eton days, was Aldous Huxley, whose successful novel *Crome Yellow* made such a great sensation when it was first published. One of the principal characters in this book was drawn from Lady Ottoline Morrell, who then lived at a house called Garsington, near Oxford, which my brother told me he had visited with

Huxley. There Lady Ottoline held court with an imposing number of writers, painters, and poets whom she delighted to encourage. She also drove about the country in a yellow phaeton. In 1930 I was acting at Sadler's Wells in a repertoire of Shakespeare plays. Lilian Baylis had only just reopened the restored theatre, where we played alternate weeks with the Old Vic in Waterloo Road, but business at the Wells was very disappointing. A tall, distinguished, but eccentric-looking lady was always conspicuous at our Saturday matinées. One could hardly fail to notice her long nose and strange horselike face, and the large brown velvet hat that she wore, like a chocolate soufflé, as she sat conspicuously among the many rows of empty seats. One day I was flattered to receive a charming note from her inviting me to tea at her house in Gower Street. With some trepidation I accepted, and found several fascinating celebrities, including Lowes Dickinson and H. G. Wells. Lady Ottoline's house, with a fine portrait of her on the staircase by Augustus John, was as individual as her strange clothes and aristocratic bearing, and that single occasion on which I was her guest made a great impression on me.

Lady Oxford was another eccentric figure whom I met on one or two occasions. I had first noticed her at a private view of the Royal Academy Summer Exhibition, to which I used to be taken by my Father when I was quite a small boy. She was then still Mrs Asquith, whose outspoken and somewhat scandalous memoirs had created a furore. As I watched her rushing about the galleries, in a feathered hat, with her hooked nose and raucous voice, I thought she resembled some maliciously hovering raven. During the Second War she lived at the Savoy Hotel, where I would pass her sitting rather disconsolately in the Grill Room, and she came to a party one night at the Apollo Theatre to celebrate the success of one of Terence Rattigan's War plays, *Flare Path*, which had been directed by her son Anthony. Here I found her in a deserted corner of the bar (where the party was being held) hunched in a low basket chair, mournfully chattering of Henry Irving. But my favourite story (told me by Frederick Ashton) is of her standing defiantly in the hall at the reception given for some smart society wedding, muttering to the guests as they arrived, 'Don't go upstairs. The bride's hideous.'

35

MUSIC-HALLS

I was never a great one for music-halls. I much preferred going to plays, and I never cared for animal acts, conjurors, ventriloquists, or clowns. Even the great Grock failed to amuse me, because he was always pretending to play the piano and never did. This trick with a musical instrument has never failed to irritate me, even with such brilliant virtuoso performers as Jack Benny and Victor Borge.

In the Twenties the 'Halls' were beginning to go downhill. The Tivoli closed in 1914, to be later re-built as a cinema. Already the Alhambra and the Empire, their famous promenades abolished, alternated variety bills with seasons of revue, ballet, and occasional straight plays and musical comedies. But the Chelsea Palace, the Palladium, The New Oxford, the Kilburn Empire, the Canterbury, and the Metropolitan in Edgware Road, still presented many of the great music-hall stars with a supporting programme of individual turns. The Hippodromes and Empires in the big provincial cities began to lose their audiences, and American bands and American star performers were hastily engaged to try to revive their popularity, as Danny Kaye and Judy Garland were to do so successfully twenty years later.

However I became a great follower of Paul Whiteman and his Band, and greatly admired Nora Bayes and Sophie Tucker when they first appeared in London. I would sometimes follow them from the Palladium to the Empire to see them twice in a single night, these double appearances being quite a usual tradition of the music-hall from the old days. Though I was rather snobbish and superior in my attitude, and inclined to scoff at the highbrow critics, who wrote such clever articles maintaining that the great variety stars were far finer artists than straight actors, I feel very grateful now for the opportunities I had of enjoying many of the most accomplished music-hall performers of the time.

I first saw Harry Tate (with Violet Loraine) in a London Hippodrome revue, *Business as Usual*. The scene was the garden of his house, 'The Nest, Tooting Bec', and I think 'Fortifying the Home' was the name of the sketch. Later at the Coliseum, in 'Fishing', he gave a madly surrealist performance (involving the idiotic fat son who always featured with him as well as a very old man) and the sketch ended with a lot of property fish, of every shape and size, whizzing about in the air on twanging fishing rods as the curtain fell. Will Hay, with his recalcitrant schoolboy class, was another favourite of mine, and the Boganny Brothers, who did a riotous sketch involving pie-throwing. There were usually some ambitious musical interludes in the respectable Coliseum programmes, Mark Hambourg playing Liszt, and a turn entitled 'Pattman and his Gigantic Organ', a title which much appealed to my schoolboy sense of humour. 'Olga, Elga, and Eli Hudson' used to give an extremely elegant presentation, appearing in full evening dress in the smartest drawing-room interior which the Coliseum could provide, with polar bear skin rugs, brocaded sofas, and tasselled lampshades. In these imposing surroundings they obliged by playing various instruments and singing popular ballads.

George Robey was often to be seen in revues and pantomimes, but his solo turn at a music-hall was on the whole more satisfactory, since he had the stage to himself and there was no need for him to pretend to defer to a partner or to try to disguise his unique personality with wigs, make-up, and characterisations. Of course he had invented his own individual get-up – the collarless long frock-coat, the big boots, and huge circular painted eyebrows. Will Fyffe and G. S. Melvin, on the other hand, excelled at mimicry and strange transformations of appearance, and I was never sure whether I would recognise them from one number to the next.

There were few funny women. Beatrice Lillie and Cicely Courtneidge had only just begun to appear as great clowns in the revues which were becoming so popular, and Gracie

Fields was touring in a revue *Mr Tower of London* with her first husband, Archie Pitt, and had not yet taken the West End by storm. But there were a few clever women mimics – Marie Dainton, for instance, and later Elizabeth Pollock and Florence Desmond, rivalled the brilliant mimics Nelson Keys and Robert Hale. The Houston sisters were a fairly broad comedy act (boy and girl) but were also rather dainty. Once I was actually on the bill with them myself at the Coliseum, where there was often one sketch or scene from the straight theatre in the programme. I had been acting as Romeo to Gwen Ffrangcon Davies's Juliet at the Regent Theatre, King's Cross, and Oswald Stoll suddenly offered us quite a large salary to perform the Balcony Scene for two weeks at the Coliseum after the Regent run had ended. Preceding us in the bill was Teddy Brown, a giant who must have weighed at least twenty stone and played the xylophone with great dexterity. As the revolving stage began to turn in order to allow our setting (an elaborate old-fashioned painted Italian garden) to be wheeled into place, the house was still loudly demanding an encore from Teddy Brown. This, needless to say, did little to increase our confidence, and I was straining every muscle in my upturned neck as I yearned towards the balcony, where Juliet, her red Botticelli wig clashing unhappily with the painted pink marble canvas balustrade on which she leaned, murmured, 'Romeo, Romeo, Wherefore art thou Romeo?' We were neither of us very sorry when the curtain fell ten minutes later to very mild applause, though of course we laboured (twice nightly) to become gradually more accustomed to the acoustics of the enormous theatre – no microphones of course in those days – and we felt we had begun to be a little more relaxed by the end of the second week of our engagement. One of the stagehands even took the trouble to tell me at the last performance that in his opinion we had much improved.

It was rather lonely in my big dressing-room behind the scenes, but I used to enjoy standing in the wings to watch the other turns. One man, a German who appeared under the name of Robbins, gave a fascinating performance without speaking a single word. He made strange noises, whispering, humming, and squeaking to himself, changing his costume all the while in front of the audience. He was dressed in layers

of strange garments which he kept changing one by one –
waistcoats, gloves, braces, trousers, belts. Everything he
wore seemed to melt away and turn into something else. And
of course from the side I could enjoy watching the way he
concealed the garments he had discarded and managed the
trick strings and fastenings which he manipulated so cleverly.
It must have been a tremendous business sorting everything
out and dressing up again in the right order for the next
performance. I made friends in those weeks with Billie and
Renée Houston, whose turn used to follow our Balcony
Scene, and the audience would roar as Billie greeted her sister
in her strong Scots accent with, 'A thousand times good
night.'

I was in front at the Coliseum more often than at any other
Variety House, and saw many great stage players there in
scenes and sketches, as well as a large number of variety
stars such as Vesta Tilley, Albert Chevalier, and Little Tich.
Seymour Hicks, Violet or Irene Vanbrugh would sometimes
be at the top of the bill, to say nothing of Sarah Bernhardt
('Between tigers, not!' Bernhardt is said to have cabled to
Stoll when he first approached her), and Ellen Terry best of
all. Bernhardt, an old woman with one leg amputated, lay,
half-covered with a cloak, at the foot of a tree as a wounded
poilu in a patriotic one-act play, but I quite believed in her
youthfulness and thrilled to the tones of the famous *voix
d'or*, even though she was reciting words that I could not
understand. And Ellen Terry, as Portia in the Trial scene, and
as Mistress Page in some excerpts from the *Merry Wives*,
enchanted me to the exclusion of everything else in the
programme.

The turns at the Coliseum were always clearly announced
by large illuminated numbers which were shown in frames
at either side of the proscenium. These numbers, though in
strict order on the printed programmes, were apt to vary at
different performances. The star turn was supposed always
to appear just after the interval, but when Gwen and I gave
our first performance we found we had been shifted to an
earlier less important place. Only after a day or two did we
discover that it was customary to send five pounds to the
stage manager if we wished to hold the top position in which
we were billed. During the one long interval the enormous

act drop would be lowered, and when I was in front I delighted in spotting the celebrities painted in a great procession on it by Byam Shaw. I found I remembered the details of the curtain very well when I found the original painting for it in a bar at the Coliseum only the other day – Ellen Terry as Beatrice kissing a mittened hand, Bernhardt as L'Aiglon, Tree as Cardinal Wolsey, John Hare, the Vanbrughs, and at least fifty other stage celebrities and opera stars of the period as well.

I only went once to the Kilburn Empire, where I was lucky enough to see Marie Lloyd shortly before she died. She wore a smart Empire dress for her first appearance, with a high diamond-topped ebony stick and some kind of elaborate head-dress with aigrettes, and sang, 'If you show the boys just a little bit, it's the little bit the boys admire,' following this with her famous charwoman number about 'The old cock linnet'. With birdcage in hand, she sank on to a park bench with very wide slats, remarking, 'Oh dear, I'm nipped in the bud.'

I never went to the Empire in Leicester Square in the days when the famous promenade permitted the 'Pretty Ladies' (as Arnold Bennett called them) to circulate and ply for custom. But after the 1914 War I often went there to enjoy all kinds of different attractions. The Astaires – Fred and Adèle – in *Lady Be Good*; George Graves and Ethel Levey in *Watch Your Step*, the first revue I ever saw ('You've been eating peas – you're rattling' he said as he put his arm round her waist). In more serious contrast was the Casson–Thorndike production of Shakespeare's *Henry the Eighth* (in which I was surprised to see each character come before the curtain to take a call – Buckingham, Wolsey, Katharine – just after they had each played a death-scene) and a spectacular failure, *Arlequin*, with Godfrey Tearle, a romantic-fantasy with an elaborate Venetian setting.

The Alhambra, too, with its twin domes and imitation Moorish architecture ornamenting Leicester Square, had a chequered career from the time of its two great First Wartime revues, *The Bing Boys* and *The Bing Boys on Broadway*. Beatrice Lillie – in top hat and tails – made one of her first successes in London there in a revue, *5064 Gerrard*, and much later, just before the theatre was pulled down (to be rebuilt as the Odeon

Cinema) a Shakespeare season was given there by Stanley
Bell, including *Henry V* and *The Merchant of Venice*. But the
Diaghilev seasons from 1919 till the early Twenties were the
great events for me. My father took me to see *Boutique
Fantasque* which had just been produced, with Massine and
Lydia Lopokova and Karsavina still dancing with the
company, while *Carnaval* and *Prince Igor* made up the rest of
the programme. Later the company moved to the Coliseum
where they would give one ballet at each variety peformance,
and there I fell madly in love with Tchernicheva, who appeared as the Swan Princess in *Children's Tale*, and *Thamar*
with its towering scenery. I would play truant from school
(Westminster), and Arnold Haskell and I would climb to the
Coliseum gallery, both of us still in our top hats (rubbed to
an effect of wet sealskin by constant use), and jam pot collars,
to see *Petrushka, Les Matelots* with Lifar, *Le Train Bleu* with
Dolin, and of course *Les Sylphides*. *The Good-Humoured Ladies*
and *Les Biches, Cléopâtre* and *Schéhérazade*, thrilled me in
another Ballet Season at the Princes Theatre (now the Shaftesbury) given with orchestral interludes by Arthur Bliss and
Stravinsky.

In 1921 came the great all star revival of *The Sleeping Princess*
at the Alhambra, and I was present on the opening night,
entranced by the splendours of the Bakst décor and brilliant
cast – Olga Spessiva as Aurora, Pierre Vladimiroff as the
Prince, Idzikowsky, Woizikowsky, Sokolova, Tchernicheva,
and Lopokova. But various disasters occurred to spoil the
evening's complete success. The magic wood refused to
grow, and Lopokova as the Lilac Fairy kept dancing to and
fro along the front of the stage waving her wand, while
ominous creakings and crackings almost drowned the orchestra. Pieces of wood emerged from the trap only to break off
or keel over after they had risen only a few inches from the
floor, and the curtain had to be lowered to cover the confusion, while in the final scene one of the dancers fell on her
back during a *pas de deux*.

I went to see the ballet many times during its short run. In
the end it lost a great deal of money, and Diaghilev was forced
to take the company abroad and leave most of the scenery
and dresses behind to cover some of his debt to Stoll, though
he did manage to salvage the décor of the last act which he

used for many years afterwards in *Aurora's Wedding*. The principals in the original Alhambra production varied on different nights, and I saw three other Auroras – Lopokova, Egorova, and Trefilova. Maria D'Albaicin, a beautiful Spaniard, was carried on in a sedan chair (ivory picked out with blue and green) to dance a slow solo variation with castanets, but *The Three Ivans* and *The Blue Bird* were perhaps the most popular items in the final Wedding scene. The King and Queen presided, though they did not dance, sitting on their thrones in tremendous grandeur, surrounded by negro attendants in magnificent Bakst uniforms. Years afterwards I was lucky enough to meet Stravinsky and his wife in New York, and recognised Mrs Stravinsky, to her great delight, as that impressive lady on the throne whose beauty I could never forget.

36

DOWN TO EARTH

It is impossible, of course, to award points to an actor or an actress as one might to a horse or a dog, a runner or a cricketer – so many marks for technical ability, so many for timing, characterisation, emotional power. The subtleties of the actor's craft are almost impossible to dissect in general terms, and any attempts to examine them in detail, except with the experienced pen of a perceptive professional writer, are apt to prove tedious and unsatisfactory to the average reader. Had I not become an actor myself, I should never have wanted to spoil my enjoyment of the theatre as a member of the audience by speculating on who should receive the final credit for an outstanding performance – author, actor, or director.

In recent years it has sometimes been suggested that rehearsals of a new play should be open to students, members of the audience, and even to the dramatic critics. I believe I speak for most of my colleagues in thinking that such a procedure would be an intolerable intrusion on the privacy of our work. Already we are bound to complete our experiments by a fixed deadline, hoping to be prepared in time, but the first performance we give in public is often greatly inferior, as we ourselves well know, to the result we can achieve after playing before an audience for several weeks. Hence the modern custom of try-outs, sometimes for more than a month, before we venture to appear in London.

In my young days first nights in the West End were apt to be extremely ragged. The prompter's voice was often much in evidence, and lighting, scene changes, and stage management were apt to go astray. This atmosphere of uncertainty, though the audience might accept it as part of the excitement of launching a new production, must have played more than usual havoc with the nerves of the players, especially in the case of the star of the company who was frequently the manager and director as well.

One evening last summer I was invited to give a talk about the theatre to a group of American students who were on a visit to London, and when, at the end, I asked for questions, a young man with a beard jumped up and demanded in rather threatening tones, 'What, in your opinion, is a star?' I circumvented him with a fairly non-committal answer, remembering too late that, when Ralph Richardson and I had been interviewed on television in America by David Frost, he had asked the same question, and Ralph had swiftly countered him by answering firmly, 'Ethel Merman'.

Was I deceived as a schoolboy into thinking that every actor or actress whose name appeared in big type was a blazing genius? Though I was lucky enough to see three great actresses, Bernhardt, Duse, and Ellen Terry, the aura of devotion which surrounded them, even in their decline, impressed me so greatly that I could not possibly, at that early age, attempt to compare their qualities or discriminate between their respective talents. I could only marvel at their staying-power and the mystique which still clung to them to the very end of their long careers. In my youth I was a wonderfully appreciative member of the audience – less so, alas, today. Though of course I imagined myself to be highly critical I suppose I was easily taken in by claptrap. But I do remember saying once, 'I wish I could have a photograph of Edith Evans. I can never recognise her when she comes on to the stage. She always looks exactly like the part she is playing.' I suppose this was really the greatest compliment I could have paid her. Of course I developed my own personal likes and dislikes and was prepared to voice them in no uncertain terms, and I did begin to realise, even when I was quite young, the difficulty that must beset a critic if he finds the mannerisms of some popular player particularly irritating or unattractive.

What is it that makes the so-called 'star'? Energy, an athletic voice, a well-graced manner, certainty of execution, some unusually fascinating originality of temperament? Vitality, certainly, and the ability to convey an impression of beauty or ugliness as the part demands, as well as authority and a sense of style.

The actor's loyalty to the playwright has certainly grown steadily during my time. In the early years of the century, Vedrenne and Barker had laboured to create good ensemble companies, and to accustom the public to appreciate them, rather than the bravura vehicles of the Victorian and Edwardian theatre, but their ventures were considered highbrow and were not really popular with the general public. Barker's Shakespeare productions at the Savoy between 1912–1914 were considered stunty and *avant-garde*, and even Shaw's plays (except for *Pygmalion* and *Arms And The Man*) appealed to a very limited audience for many years after they were written. I saw a number of them for the first time when they were given for short seasons after the Great War at the tiny Everyman Theatre in Hampstead, with splendid casts – Nicholas Hannen, Claude Rains, Edith Evans, and many other distinguished players. But *Saint Joan* was surely the first of Shaw's plays to be a big popular success.

The old-fashioned theatre manners died hard – the divisions of class in the audience, evening dress in stalls and boxes, latecomers banging down their seats, booing from the gallery if the patrons were disappointed, incidental music, receptions for the leading players, and curtain calls after every act. (Even up to 1933 this custom still prevailed and we took several bows after each act of *Richard of Bordeaux*.) Some of the artificial excitement generated by all this sense of occasion was, of course, undoubtedly genuine, and helped to make a visit to the theatre a treat for young people and a privileged hobby for the older enthusiasts, who looked upon it as a regular social event at which they were sure to meet their friends, and could discuss the play with them in the intervals, and at each other's dinner-parties in the weeks that followed.

Now of course everything is changed. Men sit in the stalls in their shirt-sleeves with their arms round the necks of their companions. They take off their shoes and put their feet up on the ledges of the boxes. But radio and television have made audiences, on the whole, more intelligently curious and better informed than they used to be, and they tend to be far more punctual as well as more attentive. If they are inclined to read newspapers while they are waiting for the play to start, their behaviour may be justified by the fact that there is now no overture to arouse their expectation, with the lights half-lowered and the footlights glowing, and the curtain is often already up when they come into the theatre. This is one of the strange new obsessions of modern directors that I have never been able to bring myself to like, though of course it is impossible to avoid it on an open stage, but in a proscenium theatre I find it a greatly disenchanting beginning to the evening.

Plays used to be clearly differentiated, and people knew just the kind of thing they wished to see, as well as the actual theatre where they were most likely to find it. Nowadays the agents and coach-parties direct their mass of patrons to a 'good show', promising either wholesome family fun or a few less savoury dishes for the stag-line. Melodrama is scarce, since it can be more richly effective in the cinema, but thrillers still seem to have their old appeal. The serious theatre, with its three main centres, The National, The Royal Shakespeare at the Aldwych, and the English Stage Company at the Court, supply rich and varied programmes, both classical and contemporary, and so do the smaller experimental houses in various parts of London. Television creates new stars. Some of them may have struggled without conspicuous success for many years in the theatre, now to be suddenly taken to the hearts of an enormous audience who might never otherwise have noticed them. The danger of this sudden success is, of course, in over-exposure, a danger equally great in the world of films and pop singing.

In the old days, the great music-hall comedians lived on the same material for their whole lives. Even if they had new songs written for them over the years, the tunes and lyrics were derived much in the same style as the old ones in which they had made their first successes. But television, radio, and piped music tend to exhaust every successful tune in a very few weeks for a larger audience than was ever imagined before, and the resulting competition has created a new world of agents and teams of gag-writers, with frenzied efforts to find new kinds of presentation, often of an abstract and surrealistic kind, which can quickly exhaust their ephemeral popularity.

How often in the past has the theatre been said to be in its last throes, yet it obstinately continues to survive. The changes that have transformed it in all its branches, especially in the last twenty years, have been violent and sudden, and it is often difficult for one to appreciate and understand them as one grows older. But I believe that there are as many great personalities today as there were in the theatre fifty years ago, and that on the whole they are considerably more generous and less selfish people than many of their predecessors used to be.

But the star of today has a very difficult task in trying to maintain some mystery, and yet to behave naturally and with some sort of modesty at the same time. The tape-recorder and the television camera can take his voice, his manner, and his face into millions of homes, while candid cameras and newshounds dog his private life when he is off the stage. But there is no doubt that the public still loves to worship actors and actresses whose personalities are strikingly original, sympathetic, or unusual, and the young adore their stage idols as well as their musical film favourites and pop singers, just as we all did in our own early theatre-going days so many years ago.

INDEX

Note: Index of principal plays and play titles.